The Drawings of Rodin

Albert Elsen
J. Kirk T. Varnedoe

The Drawings of Rodin

WITH ADDITIONAL CONTRIBUTIONS BY
VICTORIA THORSON AND
ELISABETH CHASE GEISSBUHLER

PRAEGER PUBLISHERS
New York • Washington

FRONTISPIECE. *Self-portrait*, c. 1890. Carbon pencil. 16½ x 11½ inches. Musée Rodin, Paris. Photograph by Adelys.

BOOKS THAT MATTER

Published in the United States of America in 1971
by Praeger Publishers, Inc.
111 Fourth Avenue, New York, N.Y. 10003

Library of Congress Catalog Card Number: 76–159409

Printed in the United States of America

Contents

List of Illustrations

Preface

ART HISTORY IS largely made up of detective stories. One still being written and literally involving crime is that of "Rodin Drawings, True and False." In this book, and in the exhibition at the National Gallery of Art in Washington, D.C., and The Solomon R. Guggenheim Museum in New York, we have assembled many of Rodin's best drawings that have not been seen before or have been rarely reproduced; all of them, however, are shown for the first time in approximately chronological sequence. Our purpose has been to share our discovery of Rodin's greatness as a draftsman and his astonishing range as an artist. Another purpose of the show and book was to involve scholars in a collaborative effort of mutual support rather than petty competition. We have also felt that a major public exhibition and an accompanying book drawing attention to Rodin's drawings and exposing those who for years forged Rodin's work were the appropriate and logical follow-up to Dorothy Seiberling's exposé of the Durig fakes in the June 4, 1965, issue of *Life* magazine. My own part in the Durig disclosures, and my reaction to seeing fakes reproduced and sold in galleries and auction houses and hanging in museums and private collections all over the United States and Europe, were personal motivations for the idea of the exhibition and book. Carter Brown of the National Gallery of Art and Thomas Messer of the Guggenheim Museum share my gratitude for supporting this unusual venture. I myself have been guilty of reproducing a few fake drawings years ago as a result of neglecting to give the subject the prolonged concentration and intensive study that it demands and is now receiving from Kirk Varnedoe. This project affords Mr. Varnedoe not only exposure to the disciplines of his profession but also partial publication of his doctoral thesis and the experience of working internationally with museums on a major project. The selection and organization of the exhibition, as well as of much of this book, are largely the result of his efforts. Through her contribution to this volume, Mrs. Victoria Thorson, also a doctoral student, has gained less extensive but similarly valuable experience. Mrs. Elisabeth Chase Geissbuhler, a dedicated and resourceful Rodin scholar, has demonstrated a generosity of spirit too rare in the field by contributing an essay from her own extensive researches into Rodin's architectural drawings, which will be published in the future.

Drawing and his own drawings were important to Rodin. Their exhibition and publication are intended to counter the view established by one of Rodin's secretaries and biographers that he looked upon drawings only as essays and not as works of serious art. Rodin's success as a sculptor has diverted the attention of the public from his gifts as a draftsman, something which in his own lifetime the artist took great pains to avoid. Beginning in the 1880's, he mounted several exhibitions of his drawings and showed several hundred of them in his retrospective of 1900 and at the Bernheim-Jeune Gallery thereafter. He sold and gave away countless drawings and hung them in frames by the yard in the Hôtel Biron. Several books were illustrated with his drawings, and Rodin agreed to a beautiful publication of more than 140 of his great "blacks" in 1897. Emil-Antoine Bourdelle was encouraged by the artist to write an analytical book on the drawings, a project that was unfortunately never carried out. Several appreciative articles on his sketches were written by friends and critics, and these drew his favorable response. A few years before his death in 1917, Rodin entertained the idea of a fresco in an abandoned Paris chapel.

Rodin was always concerned with preserving tangible evidence of his thought and observations, whether in letters, aphorisms dictated to secretaries, or sketches on the smallest scraps of paper. His mania for keeping his drawings was constant, and, at his death, more than 4,000 that he had retained (as counted by Judith Cladel) were transferred to the new Musée Rodin. Estimates of the number now housed in that museum range beyond 7,000.

Mrs. Geissbuhler has made the most ambitious study of hundreds of the architectural sketches and searched out their sources. Victoria Thorson introduces iconographic study of the late drawings. Kirk Varnedoe's contributions, which are the first lengthy essays based upon a systematic study of a large number of those in the Musée Rodin and throughout the world, prepare the way for their chronological dating as well as for the detection of forgeries. The prevalence of forgeries in public and private collections has cruelly discouraged extensive display, reproduction, and study of the drawings that for Rodin constituted the basis of his art and endless joy.

It is fitting that this book be dedicated to Judith Cladel for her scholarship and devotion to Rodin and particularly to his drawings. If she had been the first director of the Musée Rodin, for the inception of which she was in large part responsible, Rodin's drawings would have been more accessible, far better known, and the fakers vigorously combated until her death in 1959.

Albert Elsen
Stanford University

ACKNOWLEDGMENTS

The first part of the research leading to the essays I present here was made possible by two grants from the B. Gerald Cantor Art Foundation. I wish to express my gratitude to the Cantor Art Foundation, and to Mr. Cantor personally, for this generous support. The project was completed under the auspices of a David E. Finley Fellowship from the National Gallery of Art in Washington, D.C. I am grateful to the National Gallery for this opportunity to travel and study, and to Carter Brown, Director, Charles Parkhurst, Assistant Director, and Douglas Lewis and Grose Evans, Curators, for their help. The project could not have moved forward without the help of the staff of the Stanford University Art Department and the friendly assistance of numerous curators across the United States. The latter included Ebria Feinblatt, Harold Joachim, Victor Carlson, Alan Shestack, Clifford Dolph, and John Tancock. I extend thanks to them as well as to their counterparts in Europe, especially to Jean Adhémar of the Bibliothèque Nationale in Paris, and his assistant Claude Bourret, and to Haavard Rostrup of the Ny Carlsberg Glyptotek. Among those who shared their knowledge with me were Leo Steinberg, Dorothy Seiberling, Rodolfo Paras-Perez, Jacques de Caso, and Pat Sanders, as well as Mrs. Elisabeth Chase Geissbuhler and Victoria Thorson, co-contributors to the present volume. Their suggestions and assistance were greatly appreciated, as was the special help of Ellen Landis.

The United States Information Service, Fine Arts Division, in Paris, often helped me with matters of diplomacy. I wish to thank Gordon Wright, former cultural attaché there, and, most especially, Madame Helène Baltrusaitis, who tendered invaluable moral support as well as official aid. A special debt is owed, too, to my colleague Steve Nash, who kindly read manuscripts and provided research assistance; several of his suggestions helped to improve the final draft. In the text's preparation, the friendly support of Carol Nash and of Raymond and Annie Abella were most welcome. Research into the problem of forgeries in Rodin's drawings required, and inevitably often strained, the good will of numerous dealers and private owners. The Art Dealer's Association, through its secretary, Gilbert Edelson, supported this work, and Sotheby/Parke-Bernet cooperated to the fullest. Among private dealers, I especially thank Chuck Feingarten of Los Angeles and Claude Cueto of Paris for their help. I also hasten to offer apologies to those dealers and private collectors who suffered personally from my own lack of experience in the diplomacy of matters of inauthenticity.

In regard to source material for my research, my gratitude goes above all to Madame Cécile Goldscheider, Conservateur of the Musée Rodin, for allowing me to study large numbers of drawings from the reserve collection there, and for providing several photographs of previously unpublished drawings for illustration in the present volume. I also wish to thank her assistant Edith Lionne for her aid in my study. Mrs. E. C. Geissbuhler joins me in these acknowledgments. Finally, for his helpful criticism, his confidence in my work, and his constant, self-sacrificing endeavors to advance this research in all respects, I extend my profound gratitude to Albert Elsen.

J. KIRK T. VARNEDOE
Paris, 1971

The Drawings of Rodin

I. *Horseman*, 1880–89. Pen and ink, gouache. 8⅝ x 6¹⁵⁄₁₆ inches.
Courtesy of The Art Institute of Chicago. The Alfred Stieglitz Collection.

II. *Cambodian Dancing Girl*, 1906. Pencil, watercolor. 11⅜ x 7¾ inches.
Courtesy, Museum of Fine Arts, Boston. Bequest of John T. Spaulding.

III. *The Setting Sun (Bas Soleil)*, c. 1900–1905. Sun Series. Lead pencil, watercolor wash. 12¹⁵⁄₁₆ x 19⅞ inches.
Courtesy of The Art Institute of Chicago. The Alfred Stieglitz Collection.

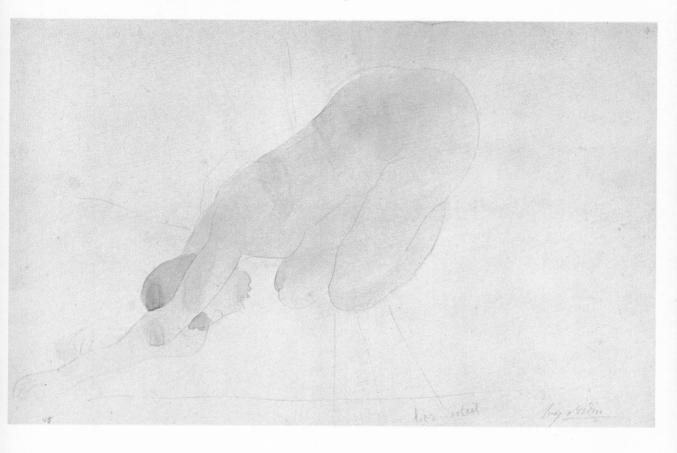

IV. *Kneeling Nude Male,* 1900–1905. Lead pencil, watercolor wash. 7¾ x 11¾ inches.
Rodin Museum, Philadelphia Museum of Art. Given by Jules Mastbaum.

Rodin's Drawings and the Mastery of Abundance

ALBERT ELSEN

WHAT DRAWING GAVE TO RODIN

DRAWING TAUGHT RODIN to see and think as an artist and helped him to make what he felt. What he saw in each human form included "secrets" and "mystery," which the act of drawing would encourage him to comprehend. A successful drawing was the result of "understanding the model," which could mean learning why as well as how a certain gesture was made. As a draftsman Rodin was a passionate reporter who could be touched by a model's "impressive movement, ravishing attitude, or right gesture which conveys a whole attitude."[1] When he said that "drawing is a perpetual comparison,"[2] he meant the matching of a drawn contour with that of the model as well as with the emotion its observation had inspired.

Almost seventy years of drawing shaped Rodin's vision, thought, and emotional life at least as much as did sculpture. Even before he became a sculptor, at about fourteen, he recognized that drawing allowed him to be an artist at all times. More lasting than his fidelity to the Church in which he was raised was his commitment to the academic dictum that drawing came first and always as a discipline and basis for form. Not by theory or history but by drawing did he learn what art was and had been, for as a student he was set to copying eighteenth-century drawings and prints, and plaster casts of ancient sculpture. It was as a drawing student that he made his first works from life outside the studio, in notebooks that he carried to the Paris streets and horse-markets, the public baths and gardens, the forested suburbs of the city, as well as to

1. Rodin drawing the Cambodian dancers in Marseille. Reproduced from *L'Illustration*, July 28, 1906.

the libraries and the Louvre. Drawing gave Rodin love as well as mastery of his métier. He was confident that it was the means of discovering "truth" in art and life. Under such teachers as Horace Lecoq de Boisbaudran, Rodin began with stubborn will and tireless ardor to discipline and coordinate hand and eye and to experience the tense concentration art demanded in order to achieve a personal expression of nature.

Medically, Rodin was myopic. Artistically, his vision had an amazing scope and depth of focus capable of discerning the subtlest detail of style or silhouette and of taking in the totality of a swift figural movement. Drawing sharpened his sight, gave him information, inspired analogies between human and natural structures, and, in short, taught him how to express knowledge. Rodin thought best when he worked. Through drawing, he memorized styles of the past, probed anatomy, and analyzed poses and their equilibrium in the work of older artists whether before his eyes or in memory ("balance is not the same in antiquity as in Michelangelo.")[3] When in the 1870's he sought to comprehend in what way his sculpture was being influenced by Michelangelo, he drew that artist's work directly and from memory and put models in Michelangelesque poses. His career as a decorative artist, his project for *The Gates of Hell*, and his love for France's artistic heritage led him to learn about architecture through drawing scores of medieval buildings over many years. His written reflections on the cathedrals largely depend upon the thought-provoking activity of his sketching. In the 1870's and 1880's, it was drawing, rather than sculpture, that prompted the freest and fullest outpouring of the passionate visions that rewarded him with self-knowledge; eventually, however, as with Cézanne, it made him distrust working from the imagination. A great deal of study directly from the model in the late 1890's, allowed Rodin to move outside of himself and to undo and rebuild his work, to analyze, to add to and recompose it—to find himself again by letting nature seem to act through his drawing.

As Rainer Maria Rilke observed, Rodin worked to master himself and his abundance.[4] At first his passion was for art, then gradually for what he felt had been the sources of the art of the Greeks, the medieval carvers, and Michelangelo: the living human body. Rodin's abundance comprised the responsiveness of his own being and artistic gifts to the legacies of art, literature, and life as he saw it.

THE RELATION OF RODIN'S DRAWINGS TO HIS SCULPTURES

Drawing did not serve Rodin as the blueprint for his sculpture. Those sketches that relate to his bronzes and marbles were made afterward as part of his continual reassessment of his work and to assist catalogue engravers. His most famous sculptural projects, such as *The Burghers of Calais*, do not seem to have called forth preliminary drawings. Nevertheless, drawing mediated between literary inspiration and personal sculptural expression, as we know from the history of *The Gates of Hell*. Through drawing, Rodin translated the *Inferno* into his own experience. The figures in the great portal trace their lineage, if not direct parentage, to hundreds of sketches inspired by meditations on Dante and Baudelaire. It is the quality of torment, agitation, struggle, and metamorphosis found in these grave drawings—not specific poses and profiles of figures and groupings—that established the emotional climate of *The Gates*. There were, in fact, times in his career when it would have been impossible for him to realize his drawings literally in sculpture. Not only his "blacks," the fantasist drawings of the late 1870's and 1880's, but also the rapid sketches of moving models and the drawings of Cambodian dancers knew no sculptural issue. Conversely, Rodin's method of constructing his sculptures by observing successive contours of the model made the single viewpoint of the drawings too limited a basis from which to model. Even when modeling, Rodin would speak of "drawing" a contour from nature. Drawing and modeling were distinct yet mutually supportive and cross-fertilizing in his art. Seeing and feeling the model's profiles through the point of his pencil and hands gave conviction to his fingering of the clay and draftsmanship. Drawing made the body's contours instinctive for the sculptor; modeling taught the draftsman what was essential.

There were practices and devices shared between the two mediums. Rarely did Rodin consider a work unalterable, and a frugality stemming from an impoverished youth led him to work over old drawings, just as he would rebuild with fresh clay an old head in plaster. He would also trace over a drawing, sometimes correcting or purifying the contours, sometimes hardly changing the line at all, in order to give a friend a copy of a sketch he wished to keep for himself. This was a process not unlike casting and editing in plaster. Tracing his own work allowed him to mask out extraneous detail, just as he would edit sculptures by amputation. Occasionally a drawn figure lacks a limb or head, which has been cut by the paper's edge, evoking Rodin's fascination with the partial figure as well as a willingness to court and preserve accidents. The change of orientation of large and small unmounted figures in his sculpture had its analogue in the drawings. Rodin would sometimes decide that he liked the expressiveness of a pose seen from a view different from that in which it was first made and would so indicate by the location of its title or the signature. There are drawings that the artist took out of their original context and remounted, conceivably because he wanted a different perspective of the pose or a better placement of the figure within the new field or, as in sculpture, he may have desired to extricate it from the context of other figures or fragmentary studies of figure parts.

Just as Rodin enjoyed surrounding himself with plaster casts of his many small figures, so he loved to review his drawings kept at hand in large folios. There were moments in his work schedule that allowed for relaxation, and he would manipulate figures and their limbs searching for a spontaneous and successful dialogue between his performers or making previously drawn contours more eloquent. There were drawings to which Rodin would add another figure, drapery, or a symbolic subject. Several possible or successive contours in a single drawing awaited these review sessions and his arbitration of their claims for supremacy. His decision would be made by a single emphatic contour remade or freshly introduced. In sculpture and drawing Rodin strove for the effect of one great certainty out of many possibilities.

WHAT ARE THE DRAWINGS ABOUT?

Thematically, Rodin's drawings are concerned with the ways men and women express themselves through the language of their bodies. Psychologically, they tell us that, for him, "The sight of human forms feeds and comforts me. I have infinite worship for the nude."[5] The early drawings from classical sculpture show his study of the body submitted to the rhetoric of the ancients, from which derived his taste for a healthy and graceful body capable of clarity of expression. Until he was forty-two, Rodin worked as a commercial decorator, and his drawings include Herculean and cherubic figures in heraldic and playful poses that he would employ in modeling a fireplace, bed, or vase decoration. The motivation for these postures of eloquent repose and athletic movement was artistic: to show the body's physical attributes to best advantage. By the same token, his youthful drawings in eighteenth-century modes show mindless figures in graceful, often playful, liaison: men, women, and children at peace with themselves. Rodin's study of Michelangelo introduced him to the body as a metaphor for serious and complex states of mind and feeling, to invented structural schemas and unnatural gestures and couplings involving many points of contact. His large number of figure drawings from the late 1870's and 1880's, predominantly male, and often gray and black in aesthetic and psychological tone, manifest his urgency to make the language of the body more expressive than beautiful. Figures are at war with themselves or are in fateful linkage. Movements are sometimes spastic, uncoordinated, and anatomically improbable, as if Rodin had sought to voice the internal passions and pressures that drive the body aimlessly. In both form and meaning, these "black" drawings imply that Rodin sought to suppress his rococo facility of hand, to strip off the gracious veneer of French taste, and to give vent to a change of thinking that was more passionate than playful.

After about 1890 Rodin drew almost exclusively from the model, who, with the exception of the trained dancer, was working in a liberated situation—liberated not only from clothing but from art postures, such as the hipshot pose automatically struck by Italian models that Rodin detested. The body language he now explored was often of a vernacular, spontaneous type. There is nothing problematic about the movements or gestures in these late drawings. Many of his subjects experience untroubled self-absorption or abandon. Rodin had embarked upon the discovery and mastery of the abundance of the body's natural movements as they could be seen in the intimacy of the studio, made by unself-conscious, often unprofessional but always expressive models. He continued to make large numbers of portrait busts and drawings of some of his subjects but came to recognize, as Rilke pointed out, that while the face is more easily readable, "life dispersed in the body was more mysterious." Detection of this mystery inspired Rodin to give up looking at his paper while drawing, so that his eyes never left the model nor pencil the paper. The resulting contours were like graphs of the model's spirit, and in them he achieved a goal shared with sculpture of imparting to the body the expressiveness of the face.

To the public unacquainted with Rodin's views on art there are drawings that may still appear perversely made to shock. His drawings after 1900 include foreshortened perspectives of reclining models with splayed legs that are at times so centered on the sheet as to be almost heraldic. For the most part, Rodin was not an artist who changed his style when treating erotic subjects, although some of the late works show a surprising aggressiveness toward the model. His drawings and sculptures that display the genitals are logical continuations not only of his style but also of his belief that any view of the human body was potentially of artistic interest and beauty. Against charges of obscenity and immorality, Rodin's defense was his sincerity of observation as an artist. Unlike his forgers, Rodin was guided by a conception of what makes a good drawing or sculpture.

REFLECTIONS ON RODIN'S STYLE

Bad drawing for Rodin was mannered and self-conscious in style. Its practitioners were poseurs, like officers who strutted in full uniform on the boulevards but shied from combat. He scorned those who would impress by the minutiae of execution, who imparted a false nobility to gesture or used pretentious poses. Insincere and inexact observation were as bad, in his opinion, as using sleights of hand to mask ignorance of nature. Good drawing showed the results of patient labor and conveyed to Rodin truth, simplicity, and the essential. Truth meant expressing not only the character of the model but also the artist's feeling, as well as the accord of the contours with each other and nature. Simplicity meant the mastery but not the elimination of details, so that one could judge quickly the rightness of the total effect. The essential included the establishment of the main figural masses and their relationships, and of the pivotal points of movement and balance, and capturing the right gesture that evoked the whole attitude.

If, as Rilke wrote, the germ of Rodin's sculpture was its surface, that of his drawing was its edge. In general, the history of his drawing moves through several stages: first, an early phase, when the edges of his figures were adroitly, if somewhat impersonally, drawn in modes acquired from the past; the next phase, when figures were established in more generalized segments according to schemas of the internal musculature of the body; then the exquisite drawings and drypoints of the 1880's in which his fluency returned, but more firm and wiry; and finally, the most personal calligraphy of the unobserved drawings and those made with a single sweeping action. The greater sketchiness of many of the late drawings Rodin justified as being a truer evocation of the general rhythm of the body in transit. "Imprecision adds to the action."[6] While academic teachers recognized this result, they considered such drawings as preliminary sketches or exercises. Rodin's practice of drawing without looking at his pencil was inspired by an obsession with capturing not just movement but, more important, the quality of *wholeness* in what he saw. He did not have to rely upon memory, and he was forced to eliminate all that was trivial in the race to fix the figure in a large, rhythmical contour. Paradoxically, Rodin's objectives were related to the ideals of academic teachers, which they were usually unsuccessful in conveying to their students. Unlike his conservative contemporaries, Rodin was able to transform his style of drawing before nature.

Whether in his drypoints, gouaches, tonal and contour pencil sketches, or watercolors, Rodin displayed a remarkable sensitivity to the physical substance of his means and its relation to the character of the represented figure or situation. "It is important that the artist be really master of his métier, that he consecrate all his resources to giving it its total expression; in a word, that he give back to the material he uses all it is susceptible to."[7] By the relative thickness of a line, its pace and inflection or response to the pressure of the hand, he established the coordination, weight, and individuality of his subject. How often we see in Rodin's work qualities of drawing that go beyond the mimetic to the poetic.

When Rodin adopted watercolor after 1900, both of these purposes were served. The addition of a color allowed him literally to flesh out a contour drawing and make the body's mass more palpable. The truth of volumes described by the lines could be verified. He could also put his "environment" *within* the contours of his figure, which was then seen against an empty background. Watercolor was another means by which Rodin could realize the plenitude of the model, which is what he meant when he praised the "fullness" and "expressiveness of nature." After 1900, he came to revel in strongly contrasting saturated colors, which heightened the decorative appeal of the work.

Rodin's drawings stand out from those of his forgers by virtue of his greater understanding and command of balance—they "carry," and the figure holds its place within the field of the drawing. A thorough comprehension of the body's internal structure, its reflexive self-balancing in the response to gravity during the most strenuous movement, and the points that carry the weight always inform Rodin's drawings. Even when he inverted a finished drawing to give us a flying figure, we can read the original pose and the body's response to gravity.

WHAT RODIN GAVE TO DRAWING

Rodin's drawings, as much as his sculpture, confirm his remoteness from Impressionism and his independence from late-nineteenth-century styles in painting. His "blacks," developed during the height of Impressonism, are totally alien to that movement in their passionate and strident themes, somber tonalities, and unflinching linearity. To draw naturally and simply was his personal creed until his death, and his unwillingness to stylize his art separated him from fin-de-siècle movements, such as *art nouveau*, with their emphasis upon artifice and deviation from the natural in form and subject. Superficially, his drawings lacking shading or ground line would seem to link his art with the surface emphasis of many artists working at the end of the last century and early in this one. The modern feeling of simplicity in his late drawings evolved from a hard-earned economy and a thoughtful understanding of what was essential and did not derive from external influence. Rodin made no concession to the flatness of his drawing paper when it came to establishing the contour of his model. *He always saw and rendered the model in depth.* The distortions in anatomy and proportion that came with not looking at his drawing and from the speed of execution in the late work, do not make him an Expressionist. They result from direct observation and feeling induced by vision rather than a mood or imagination. Artists as divergent as Matisse, Kokoschka, and Schiele looked long and knowingly at Rodin's many exhibited and published drawings and surely learned much from them. These artists fulfilled Rodin's ideal of developing a personal vision based upon continual contact with nature and of drawing without affectation.

Rodin did not consider himself a revolutionary in sculpture or drawing. Conservatism was persistently interwoven into the fabric of his thinking about art; even after 1900, he could make sculptures of a muse or make a drawing from an anonymous model into a symbolic personage. For much of his life, his attitude toward his audacities in these media was ambivalent. As with the partial figure, Rodin took many years to consider his drawings as important and self-sufficient or complete as works of art.

Looked at in retrospect and in terms of his influence, Rodin gave to drawing renewed dignity, vitality, and importance as an art form. Rejecting the grand style, he uncomplicated drawing by his insistence on being natural and striving for the simple without loss of character. He brought a sexual candor to the rendering of the body in serious drawing that was not lost on such artists as Schiele, Pascin, and Matisse. His daring mode of reporting with his pencil often stressed expressiveness over anatomical beauty and correct proportion. Drawing was crucial to the artist's self-affirmation, and Rodin's own work in this medium was given strength by the passion to see, to know, and to feel.

NOTES

1. In Albert Elsen (ed.), *Auguste Rodin: Readings on His Life and Work* (Englewood Cliffs, N.J.: Prentice-Hall, 1965), p. 172.

2. *Ibid.*, p. 176.

3. *Ibid.*, p. 162.

4. *Ibid.*, p. 116.

5. *Ibid.*, p. 164.

6. *Ibid.*, p. 163.

7. *Ibid.*, p. 174.

Rodin as a Draftsman— A Chronological Perspective

J. KIRK T. VARNEDOE

INTRODUCTION

"DRAWING," RODIN TOLD Judith Cladel in 1914, "is the key to knowledge."[1] For all Rodin's creative life, drawing was a sister process to thought; he believed that only continual drawing could train the perceptive abilities and provide the knowledge essential to development. To another friend, he asserted that "only the knowledge of drawing permits one to compare, judge, express simplicity in fixing the essential . . . without drawing, no truth."[2]

The statement recorded by Cladel could be paraphrased as a guideline for admirers of Rodin's work: The artist's own drawings are a key to fuller knowledge of his art. The use of this key, however, depends on our ability to treat graphic and sculptural production integrally, and this ability in turn depends on the establishment of an effective chronology within the graphic *oeuvre*.

Rodin's drawings have been inadequately chronicled, although the order of his sculpted works is relatively well-established; this is understandable in terms of a few major problems. First, though the body of extant works is enormous,[3] solid points of reference are few. Rodin only rarely published or exhibited drawings prior to 1897, and preparatory drawings that can be directly related to sculptures are practically unknown. Only a small number of sheets bear written dates, and such dates as do exist invariably signal the occasion on which the works were given

25

away, rather than the time of their creation; hence these can only be taken as *termini ante quem*.[4]

Second, though Rodin saved drawings from every period of his life, his practice of reworking and re-using them tends to confuse any attempt to establish a linear order. Third, the tendency to subsume earlier works in later styles or contexts was paralleled by the artist's retention of several widely different graphic manners that he could and did employ simultaneously, depending on the medium and the subject.

Such complicating factors will always obstruct absolute accuracy in dating specific drawings; however, recent research, especially among unpublished drawings at the Musée Rodin in Paris, makes it possible to offer a more complete and detailed outline of the artist's development as a draftsman, in the hopes of establishing a working guide to further study in this field.

1854–64

Léonce Bénédite, a friend of the sculptor and the first curator of the Musée Rodin, stated that Rodin had even preserved copies drawn in his pre-school years.[5] Though it is possible that a recently published drawing justifies this claim,[6] satisfactory documentation of Rodin's art begins only in 1854, at the end of his reputedly painful and unproductive academic education.[7] In that year, at the age of fourteen, Rodin began his training as a draftsman and painter at the Special Imperial School of Drawing and Mathematics, then known as the Petite Ecole (Little School) to distinguish it from the larger, more prestigious fine arts academy, the Ecole des Beaux-Arts; admission to the latter was by competition only, whereas the former was open to students and artisans at all levels. Rodin also practiced drawing at the life-drawing studio of the Gobelins tapestry works, and the Museum of Natural History, and independently at the Louvre and in the print room of the Imperial Library.[8]

Rodin may have been thinking of his own work when he later stated, "an artist's first drawings show germinally all his qualities and all his faults."[9] From our own perspective, however, it is difficult to find such firm indications amid the stylistic diversity of his early works. Although there were various traditions of draftsmanship available as models for the student of Rodin's time, no one manner held sway. Furthermore, the Petite Ecole was primarily a training ground for the industrial arts, and Rodin was spared the necessity of strict obedience to the more doctrinaire tenets of official fine-arts instruction. Moreover, because he was at first destined for a career as a practician or commercial artist's assistant, the ability to design fluently in a variety of styles would have been a prime goal of his training. Finally, the particularly willful permissiveness of the

Petite Ecole's most important instructor, Horace Lecoq de Boisbaudran, was a crucial element in Rodin's student experience.[10]

Though some of Lecoq's mechanical methods were similar to those used in other art schools, his teaching was free from the biases that accompanied instruction elsewhere. Whether training his students in usual or innovative drafting procedures, Lecoq insistently avoided imposing a moral value-scale of style, and held that it was the role of the artist to bring out the beauty inherent in all aspects of nature.

Given the freedom of expression stressed by Lecoq, the variety of Rodin's student works suggests that he passed these years free not only from the external constraints of orthodoxy but also from the internal focusing impulse of personal maturity. The lack of the former and the slow arrival of the latter in no way detracted from his facility but defined an individuality characterized by free experiment rather than decisive singlemindedness.

Rodin's earliest copy exercises show that his point of departure was fairly standard. Albert Boime, in his study of the drawing instruction in the academic studios and schools of the nineteenth century, points out a variety of student techniques, most of which are found in Rodin's early drawings preserved at the Musée Rodin.[11] Lecoq encouraged his students to learn by copying from prints and drawings—a practice that, though widely followed, was looked upon with disfavor in the Ecole des Beaux-Arts itself;[12] in following this practice, Rodin worked in a variety of styles whose origins lay in reproductive graving techniques. Most prominent among these is a linear articulation in which volumes are indicated by restressed contours, and shading with parallel lines. This is seen in a series of pen and sepia studies of Parthenon sculpture (*Fig. 2*).[13]

The most proficient of the artist's student copies, including a series of fine-line pencil studies washed with pale watercolor tones, show that he was increasingly attracted to late-antique models. Scenes such as that in the stomped-pencil copy in Figure 3 are based on antique vase decorations, but Rodin appears to have studied them through eighteenth- or nineteenth-century reconstructions, with added spatial and coloristic effects, rather than in original form.[14]

Exposure to Lecoq's controversial course in the training of the visual memory aided Rodin in his study of the art of the past; he painted from memory copies of works studied in museums, and he preserved at least two drawings that reflect his practice in this area. Copies after Eustache Le Sueur's *Jesus Carrying the Cross* and *The Infancy of Bacchus* by Poussin, they display an undetailed, bland tonal facture, with little feel for line or volume.[15]

No known drawings, however, give evidence that Rodin attended Lecoq's special outdoor sessions for advanced students, where models moved around without set pose; here the students could make quick

2. *Fragment of the Panathenaic Procession* (copy of the Parthenon frieze), c. 1854–55. Pen and sepia ink. 4¹⁄₁₆ x 6¾ inches. Musée Rodin, Paris (no. 62). Photograph by Adelys.

3. *Bacchic Procession*, c. 1858. Lead pencil. 9³⁄₁₆ x 9¹⁄₁₆ inches. Musée Rodin, Paris (no. 324). Photograph by Adelys.

4. *Study of Nude Model*, c. 1857–59. Black carbon
pencil. 23⅞ x 17⅞ inches. Musée Rodin, Paris
(no. 5104). Photograph by Adelys.

5. *Study of Nude Model*, c. 1857. Black carbon
pencil. 22⅞ x 16⅜ inches. Musée Rodin, Paris
(no. 5102). Photograph by Adelys.

sketches that would later be used to produce a finished drawing with the aid of the trained memory. The eight early life-drawings now known show, instead, standard academic poses.[16] In these, as in his copies, Rodin experimented with different manners, ranging from a heavily stomped, smooth tonal facture (*Fig. 4*), to a more textured stylization reminiscent of such eighteenth-century draftsmen as Carl Van Loo, whose work Rodin is known to have copied (*Fig. 5*). Though inconsistent in quality as well as technique (they were apparently done over a period of years) the ensemble of Rodin's life studies contains several very strong exercises. At least one (*Fig. 4*), prefigures the technique of Rodin's later charcoal work, with a skillful modeling up to the highlights, a ground heightened with strong, free hatchings, and an effective combination of stomped toning and bolder outline strokes. Its quality serves to remind us that, in his three efforts to gain entrance to the Ecole des Beaux-Arts (between 1857 and 1859), Rodin was accepted in drawing, though not in sculpture. The artist later told a journalist that, before he left the Petite Ecole "he could draw from the living model as well as ever he could."[17]

We may also attribute to this period a series of careful drawings after human and equine skeletal and muscular systems (*Fig. 6*),[18] researches into the subsurface of life forms. Such study of anatomy was normal in any student curriculum; for Rodin, however, the practice was restressed by his work at the Museum of Natural History under the tutelage of the animal sculptor Antoine Barye. Later recollections allow us to connect some studies of fragments of animal anatomy with this instruction, and to this period we may also assign a series of life studies of wild animals (*Fig. 7*).[19]

This latter appears in one of the most complete records of Rodin as a young draftsman, a sketchbook given by the artist to his cousin and later purchased for the Mastbaum Collection of Philadelphia.[20] Judith Cladel, who attempted to get the sketchbook back for Rodin near the end of his life, wrote the following outline of its history:

> Rodin filled this little album with drawings between the ages of 16 and 18. It bears witness to the diversity of the studies the artist pursued then. These are sketches taken down in the course of walks in Paris, on the corners of the streets, at the Horse-Market in the Boulevard Saint-Marcel, and a few landscapes from the Paris area. Others were done at the Museum, under the tutelage of the great Barye, and in front of the cages of the wild animals; still others were executed after some painting or sculpture, or certainly after a work on "Costume in Antiquity" which Rodin consulted at the library of the Louvre.[21]

Despite some notable discrepancies (Rodin studied under Barye at the Museum when he was twenty-three to twenty-four years of age); Miss Cladel's characterization is generally accurate; the book should be dated at the end of the early period, about 1863–64.[22] The images in this album should be especially valuable, as they represent Rodin's private work, whereas the drawings considered up to this point appear to have been carefully conceived exercises or presentation pieces.[23] The pages do breathe a greater spontaneity than most of Rodin's student works, and the quick studies of horses in the street (*Fig. 8*) show the beginnings of his fascination with the transcription of unbounded movement into art. It must be admitted, however, that the ensemble presents little that reflects the future artist. These are works of immaturity, seemingly individualized only by an idiosyncratic figure type (*Fig. 9*).

But the sketchbook, taken as a whole, can be seen to imply certain aspects of Rodin's life at the time. For example, though the drawings have nothing in common with Jean-Baptiste Carpeaux's graphic work of this date, they do suggest certain parallels between Rodin and Carpeaux, a prominent sculptor of the 1860's who had been an instructor at the Petite Ecole.[24]

When speaking later of Carpeaux, Rodin noted especially the birthplace he shared with Watteau (Valenciennes, in northern France); he saw correctly that Carpeaux's forceful romanticism was heavily laced with a heritage of eighteenth-century grace.[25] The Mastbaum sketchbook shows us that Rodin imbibed a similarly mixed brew. The attenuated, high-waisted proportions, delicate extremities, and excessively contrapuntal postures of many of the figures (*Figs. 9 and 10*) point to the influence of the French eighteenth century, in which the Petite Ecole was steeped, while the tossed hair and agonized expression on page 1 (*Fig. 10*), the thematic interest in wild animals and charging equestrians (*Figs. 7 and 11*), and certain passages of calligraphically active line (*Fig. 12*) all combine to signal a nascent romantic impulse. The latter is even more evident in a series of small sepia copies after Arab street scenes, preserved in the Musée Rodin (*Fig. 13*).[26]

The eighteenth-century overtones in the sketchbook doubtless owe much to the Petite Ecole. They may also have some basis in the early development of Rodin's personality, in that a certain effeminancy, concomitant with a delayed physical maturation, may have initially figured in his attraction to the graces of the rococo period; a delicate pencil self-portrait of about 1858 suggests that this is so.[27] But, in a broader and more important sense, this strain in the sketchbook, and in Rodin's early art, corresponds to his involvement with the contemporary eighteenth-century revival among sculptors. The Petite Ecole was a training ground for this trend, for its pupils included not only Jules Dalou and Rodin in the 1850's, but also, in the 1840's, Carpeaux himself and the "Clodion of the Second Empire," Albert-Ernest Carrier-Belleuse, a popular decorative sculptor whose assistant Rodin would soon become. Though these men were not without success in academic circles (Carpeaux won the coveted Prix de Rome in 1854), the trend moved largely without the sanc-

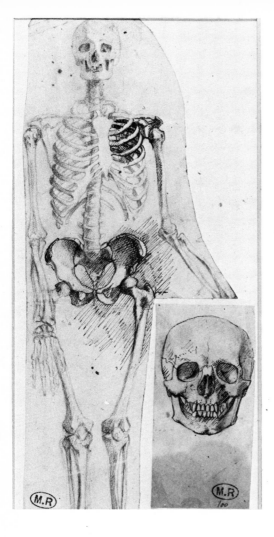

6. (a) *Skull*, c. 1856. Pen and ink over pencil.
4 1/16 x 1 7/8 inches. Musée Rodin, Paris (no. 100).
(b) *Skeleton*, c. 1856. Pen and ink over pencil.
10 x 2 3/16 inches. Musée Rodin, Paris (no. 102).
Photograph by Adelys.

7. *Leopard*, c. 1863–64. Lead pencil, sepia ink.
3 3/4 x 5 7/8 inches. Mastbaum Sketchbook, p. 24,
recto. Collection of Mrs. Jefferson Dickson,
Beverly Hills.

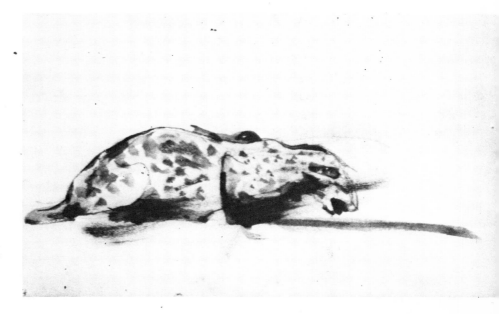

8. *Horse and Carriage*, c. 1863–64. Lead pencil. 3¾ x 5⅞ inches. Mastbaum Sketchbook, p. 4, verso. Collection of Mrs. Jefferson Dickson, Beverly Hills.

9. *Studies*, c. 1863–64. Lead pencil, pen and sepia ink, wash. 3¾ x 5⅞ inches. Mastbaum Sketchbook, p. 20, recto. Collection of Mrs. Jefferson Dickson, Beverly Hills.

10. *Nude Male Figure*, c. 1863–64. Pen and ink. 3¾ x 5⅞ inches. Mastbaum Sketchbook, p. 1, recto. Collection of Mrs. Jefferson Dickson, Beverly Hills.

11. *Two Equestrian Figures*, c. 1863–64. Pen and sepia ink, wash. 3¾ x 5⅞ inches. Mastbaum Sketchbook, p. 19, recto. Collection of Mrs. Jefferson Dickson, Beverly Hills.

12. *Nude Male Figure*, c. 1863–64. Pen and
sepia ink. 3¾ x 5⅞ inches. Mastbaum Sketchbook, p. 18, recto (detail). Collection of Mrs.
Jefferson Dickson, Beverly Hills.

13. *Arab Street Scene*, c. 1860–63. Pen and sepia ink. 2¹¹⁄₁₆ x 3⅝
inches. Musée Rodin, Paris (no. 177). Photograph by Adelys. *Actual
size.*

tion of official doctrine. This situation, indeed, was responsible for Rodin's failure to gain entrance to the Ecole des Beaux-Arts, as his competition sculptures, in an eighteenth-century vein, were too loose and too supple in facture to suit the neoclassically inclined academicians.[28] The aspect of the eighteenth century undergoing revival was that of Clodion, especially as embodied in his active, crisp terra cottas; and, beyond the question of appealing profitably to a popular taste for its attendant frivolities, Rodin and others involved found the more liberal facture and pervasive eroticism of this artistic ambiance to be a congenial milieu for the production of more expressive art.[29]

It should not be surprising, then, to find romantic tendencies in the work of some of the same artists—Carpeaux being a prime example. Rodin's contact with romanticism in sculpture was not limited to his brushes with Carpeaux and Barye, however, but extended to two other important figures in his early life: Hippolyte Maindron, the sculptor who in 1857 convinced Rodin's father to allow him to pursue an artist's career, and Jules Klagmann, a figural sculptor for whom Rodin worked about 1860.[30]

We can detect in the Mastbaum sketchbook implications of this mixed environment in which Rodin moved. But the various inflections in the manner of drawing make a blend that is neither a direct imitation of any traditional mode nor a reflection of any particular instructor. None of the powerful figures under whose aegis Rodin passed in these years left an immediate, enduring stamp on his manner, though the influence of each was reasserted later. Stylistic imitation of Lecoq would have been impossible, as the master scrupulously avoided showing his own work to students;[31] furthermore, it is clear that Rodin was not one of Lecoq's special pupils, despite a record of some success at the school.[32] It was only as he matured that Rodin fully exploited all the methods that constituted Lecoq's unorthodox curriculum.

The exercises in memory-training were of enormous importance to Rodin in later years. His most significant immediate debt to his teacher, though, was a dedication to the study of nature and to the nonchanneled development and expression of his individual spirit, in whatever mode or variety of modes he found appropriate. Lecoq insisted on the latter as the cornerstone of his instruction, and, writing in 1862, he capitalized each letter in these words for emphasis: "Art is essentially individual—individuality makes the artist. All instruction, to be true and rational, should propose to conserve, to develop, and to perfect the individual spirit of the artist."[33] Rodin, reflecting later on the years at the Petite Ecole, realized their importance in precisely these terms. They were, he said, "the germinating period of my life, where my own nature planted itself without let or hindrance; where the seeds of my subsequent development were sown; and where I received the only instruction of my life."[34]

1864–75

The year 1864 marked a turning point in Rodin's life. Having undergone a religious crisis following the death of his sister Maria in 1862, he spent several months in a monastic order. On leaving the cloister, Rodin established his first studio, and was joined there in 1864 by the girl who became his companion for life, Rose Beuret. In the same year he made his first attempt at entering a work in the Salon, *The Man with the Broken Nose.*

Though it seems that Rodin came to maturity and independence at about this time, his development as an artist remains largely hidden from view for some while, and particularly before his move to Belgium in 1870. He became an assistant to Carrier-Belleuse in 1864, and worked for him, off and on, until 1872, after which time he formed a brief partnership with a Belgian sculptor.

During this period, Rodin sculpted several major figures on his own (no trace remains of them). They were greatly affected by his drafting background, as he explained: "I drew a lot before beginning to model; in order to do the best possible, ever since my first study, I applied naïvely to clay whatever I knew of drawing, and that led me to see contours, to understand and transcribe them."[35] He also studied extensively from life, in an effort to counteract the injurious facility required of him on the job;[36] yet no known drawings document either the statues or this study. It is initially perplexing that, in comparison to the number of student works preserved, no drawings readily attach themselves to the period of Rodin's apprenticeship in Paris and Brussels.

Documentation for this period may be found, however, if we reexamine a large number of the artist's so-called "Dantesque" drawings. These latter (Figures 14, 15, and 16 are examples) are most frequently associated with the years of Rodin's work on *The Gates of Hell,* a portal commissioned in 1880 for a projected Musée des Arts Decoratifs in Paris. *The Gates,* retained unfinished by Rodin until his death, were to represent scenes from Dante's *Divine Comedy.* Thus, a certain logic supports the idea that the dramatic visions of struggle and violence, and the cruelties of the *Inferno* were the result of the portal project. However, two prominent Rodin scholars have suggested that many such drawings could have been done before 1880.[37] Following their lead with new study of the drawings themselves, this chronology offers the hypothesis that such drawings as Figures 14, 15, and 16, and related images such as Figures 18, 38, 39, and 40, may be explained as follows: As the records of experimentation and study in the 1860's and 1870's, Rodin saved many sheets such as that illustrated in Figure 14. Generally in pencil, or pen and sepia, these are called, generically, the "Dantesque" drawings, though they are of diverse thematic inspiration. In the later 1870's, and especially in connection with the stimulus of *The Gates* commission in

15. *Ugolino—The Cruel Repast*, c. 1870–80. Pencil, pen and ink. 6 x 7¾ inches. Rodin Museum, Philadelphia Museum of Art. Given by Jules Mastbaum.

14. *Group of Figures,* c. 1870. Lead pencil. 5 x 6¹¹/₁₆ inches. Musée Rodin, Paris (no. 401). Photograph by Adelys.

16. *Three Figures with Tambourine,* c. 1880–82. Pencil, watercolor wash. 5 x 3¾ inches. Rodin Museum, Philadelphia Museum of Art. Given by Jules Mastbaum. *Actual size.*

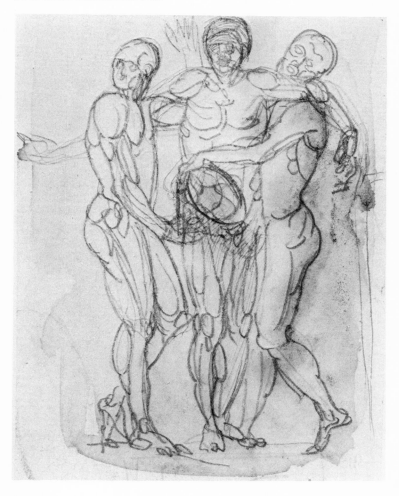

1880, Rodin directly reworked many of these drawings. Reworking with ink, sepia, and gouache, in response to a concern for more decisive line, denser modeling, and more tenebristic effects, produced images such as Figures 18, 38, 39, and 40. These have been called Rodin's "black" drawings, both because of their violent content and their dramatic effects of light.

Such a hypothesis by no means denies the existence of numerous drawings produced entirely in the 1880's. It suggests only that the beginnings of the so-called "Dantesque" mode, and in many cases the first levels of graphic work in many of the "black" gouached drawings, may be assigned to an earlier period (1864–75) than has generally been accepted. As the "Dantesque" drawings immediately follow the student works in the preserved *oeuvre*,[38] and as the size of the Musée Rodin collection proves Rodin to have been a constant conservator of his own work, such a re-evaluation is logically in order.

It is highly likely that, as a developing artist, Rodin constantly experimented with figure poses and compositions. Especially given the limited time and money available to him, drawing would have been a major means of realizing his ideas. "Though I was making poor sculpture for Belleuse," he later remarked, "I was always thinking to myself about the composition of figures, and this helped me later on."[39]

The connection of all of Rodin's imaginative drawings with Dante, and thus with *The Gates* commission, is certainly incorrect. Many drawings now reworked as separate thematic units, under varying titles, were originally simply fragments of sheets of random posture studies;[40] there also exist, among the "Dantesque" scenes, specific thematic references to other iconographies, notably Christian.[41]

Even drawings of unmistakably Dantesque reference (*Fig. 15*) may have been done well before 1880. In 1876, Rodin sculpted an *Ugolino*, which he subsequently destroyed.[42] His exposure to the theme can be dated much earlier: Carpeaux's *Ugolino* was exhibited in Paris in 1862, and, since the 1850's, Rodin had been reading Dante.[43] Furthermore, Jules Klagmann, under whom Rodin worked and studied around 1860, was a devotee of Dante, and may have passed along his enthusiasm. Even in the years before the Petite Ecole, Rodin was in the habit of drawing the creatures of his imagination, and it is unlikely that the impress of his readings did not take visible form.[44]

True to the practices of his time, Rodin cloaked his imaginative projects in traditional compositions familiar to him through his study of the art of the past. The huddled personage on the right in Figure 15 is derived from the mourning figures traditionally found in deathbed scenes dating back to antiquity, and the composition includes entombment scenes in its ancestry.[45]

The origins of the style of rendering are more obscure. Where the initial work of early imaginative drawings remains exposed to view, as in Figure 14 and parts of Figure 15, we can see that the bodies are built up in short, stabbed strokes, stressing discontinuity in the separate protrusions of muscles and bones. Some of the pencil drawings of the "Dantesque" group seem technically infantile in their heavy-handedness. This willful crudeness, evident to some extent in Figure 14, does not appear to derive from external models, and may represent the artist's earliest efforts to develop a more uniquely personal manner.

The imaginative drawings were conceived in a separate mode (compare them to the Mastbaum sketchbook) that continued unchanged in some of its features into the late 1880's. The mode is characterized by bulky, muscular bodies, often displaying a "flayed" anatomy (*Fig. 16*), and by constricted compositions in which the figures fill the space in the manner of a bas-relief.[46] Later reworkings (in the case of Figure 15, shading with parallel pen strokes) tend to unify disjointed contours and solidify the major masses of the form. This increased fluidity was later subsumed into the mode itself, as can be seen in Figure 16 (which dates around 1880, or somewhat after).

Pen and wash reworkings of early imaginative drawings apparently occurred frequently, even before the emergence of the fully developed "black" gouached style. It is clear that some preserved fragments were heightened with wash prior to being torn from larger sheets. Figure 17 is typical of these, and its thick, blocky wash contours probably correspond to a time close to the drawing's conception.[47] More frequently, though, reworkings of the "Dantesque" drawings reveal themselves by the continuation of a line or wash from the original sheet onto its mounting; this tends to suggest a broad interval between initial conception and revision. Many of Rodin's gouached drawings, normally dated wholly in the 1880's, show obvious examples of such two-sheet facture; the *Medea* (*Fig. 18*) and the *Horseman* (*Color Plate I*) are typical. The question of how much earlier to date the original sheets may always remain uncertain. Georges Grappe, a curator of the Musée Rodin, stated that not one of the "Dantesque" sheets is dated, but he asserted, nevertheless, he had "no compunction in affirming that the earliest of the ink drawings go back to 1865, if not earlier."[48]

In support of this conclusion is an important and inexplicably neglected article by Camille Mauclair, an author who talked at length with Rodin, and whose writings were sometimes the product of collaboration with the artist.[49] Discussing Rodin's sculptural production after 1880, Mauclair stressed the importance to Rodin of the compositional thinking done in the late 1860's and in the 1870's:

One must assign to the period between 1867 and 1877 three-quarters of all that has been seen of Rodin's sculpture. Certain works waited fifteen years to be executed in three months from a previous sketch. . . .

It is thus in this ten-year period that the technique and the ideology of Monsieur Rodin were formed together, and it is then that one must date the underlying construction of which his revealed works have been only the results. He had foreseen everything and has invented nothing 'from scratch' except since 1897.[50]

Mauclair's statement should not be taken to mean that specific drawings always led to specific sculptures, though in one or two instances this seems to have been the case.[51] However, it does support the contention that the researches of the 1860's and 1870's were the basis from which Rodin moved on to produce the work of the 1880's. Taking the plausible assumption that such researches involved frequent drawings, the early "Dantesque" drawings may be seen to correspond to the period of study, and the more fully achieved gouached versions to embody the assimilation of that study into new ideas and new techniques.

1875–80

Mauclair speaks of 1867–77 as the period of preparation for Rodin. In terms of a chronology of drawings, however, we should consider the two years after 1875 separately, as a part of the period in which a new influence provoked the definitive consolidation, re-evaluation, and often physical reconstitution of the artist's previous work. Mauclair himself identified the new influence and indicated the justness of this separate consideration when he reported in the same article: "With regard to the Renaissance, and especially Michelangelo, Monsieur Rodin acknowledges that he only drew profitable instruction from that source after a trip to Italy in 1875, and from that point truly dates his theory of amplification in its definitive form."[52]

Before 1875, Rodin knew Michelangelo's work largely through intermediary artists. The caryatids designed for Brussels' Boulevard Anspach in 1874, for instance, are Michelangelesque but derive more specifically from Pierre Puget's caryatids on the Hôtel de Ville, in Toulon, and perhaps even more directly from other intervening sources.[53] Certainly, a Michelangelesque spirit had been involved in the earlier imaginative drawings but not in a consistent, systematically imitative way. "I had always admired Michelangelo," Rodin commented on the period before 1875, "but I saw him at a great distance."[54]

The turning point came during work on an Antwerp monument in 1874, in which one particular figure (of a sailor) emerged in a new fashion. "My studies had been a blind search after the movement of figures," the artist said, "and in making this one, I was, for the first time, impressed with its resemblance to the compositions of the great

Florentine."[55] His curiosity piqued, Rodin set out in 1875 for Italy to see Michelangelo at first hand.

The figures of the Medici tombs in the sacristy of San Lorenzo were the greatest revelation to Rodin; his chief aid to understanding was drawing, used in a special fashion. In an attitude probably rooted in the memory exercises of Lecoq's training, Rodin chose not to work directly from the statues but instead used the act of drawing as a test; rather than seeking to record their appearance, he evolved a series of constructs with which he hoped to seize the underlying compositional principles.

> After looking at these figures long and well, I returned to my room at the hotel and began making sketches, to test the depth of my own capacity of composition and of the impressions I had received; and I found that I could do nothing like my sailor, unless I copied Michelangelo. I made no end of sketches, always with the same result. During my journey to Rome, Naples, Siena, and Venice, I continued drawing, in the hope of discovering the principles upon which the composition of Michelangelo's figures were founded.[56]

A letter written by Rodin from Florence further clarifies the nature of these drawings. "Everything that I have seen of photographs or plasters gives no idea at all of the sacristy of San Lorenzo. These tombs must be seen in profile, in three-quarters. . . . I have made sketches at night, in my hotel, not after the works, but after all the scaffolding, the systems I construct in my imagination in order to understand them."[57] As Albert Alhadeff has correctly pointed out, this letter strongly suggests that the large studies of the tomb figures in the Musée Rodin (*Figs. 19 and 20*) do not date from this encounter.[58] Alhadeff believes them to be student works, though two of Rodin's contemporaries dated them in 1877, after his return to Paris.[59] Both accounts may be partially correct;[60] in any event, it seems certain that they were done from casts of the tomb figures available in Paris (plasters that Rodin's letter, above, indicated that he knew), rather than *in situ*.[61]

Though none of the structural researches mentioned by Rodin have been identified to fill the gap left by the exclusion of these larger drawings, the Musée Rodin does possess three *in situ* sketches of the tomb of Lorenzo de' Medici itself corresponding to the mentioned attraction for side and three-quarter viewpoints (*Fig. 21*).[62] These form part of several montage sheets of drawings, including thirty-three pages or page fragments from a sketchbook used during the trip.[63] The San Lorenzo studies were not done in this little album, but among its fragments are studies of Michelangelo's *Leda*, also in Florence, and of the *Moses* (*Fig. 22*) and *Rachel* from the tomb of Julius II in Rome; there is also one other small sketch of a wall of the San Lorenzo sacristy on a separate sheet of architectural notations.[64]

17. *Movement (Caryatid)*, c. 1870–75. Pencil, gouache. 10¾ x 5⅞ inches. Collection of Mr. and Mrs. Charles Solomon, Philadelphia.

18. *Medea*, c. 1880. Ink, gouache, sepia over lead pencil. 7⅝ x 5¼ inches. Collection of Mrs. Jefferson Dickson, Beverly Hills.

19. *Study of Michelangelo's "The Medici Madonna,"* c. 1857 (?). Brown chalk. 23 x 16⅞ inches. Musée Rodin, Paris (no. 5116).

20. *Study of Michelangelo's "Dawn,"* 1877. Charcoal. 23 x 18⅛ inches. Musée Rodin, Paris (no. 5117).

21. *Study of Michelangelo's "Dawn,"*
1875. Lead pencil. 4⅜ x 2⅝ inches.
Musée Rodin, Paris (no. 270). *Actual
size.*

22. *Study of Michelangelo's "Moses,"*
1875. Lead pencil. 2¹⁵⁄₁₆ x 2⅝ inches.
Musée Rodin, Paris (no. 192). *Actual
size.*

23. *Group of Life Studies*, 1875–76. Lead pencil. 8¹³⁄₁₆ x 11¾ inches. Musée Rodin, Paris (nos. 280–84).

24. *Group of Life Studies*, 1875–76. Lead pencil. 8¹³⁄₁₆ x 11¾ inches. Musée Rodin, Paris (nos. 285–88).

25. *Figure in Pose of Michelangelo's "Apollo,"* 1875–76. Gouache over lead pencil. 13¼ x 9 inches. Maryhill Museum of Art, Maryhill, Washington.

26. *Assemblage of Two Traced Figures,*
1875–76. Pen and ink, sepia. 5 inches high.
Musée Rodin, Paris (no. 305). Photograph
by Adelys.

27. *Vase of the Elements,* 1879. Lead
pencil. 9¼ x 6⅜ inches. Collection of
Mr. Enoch Light, New York.

In order to incorporate into his work the knowledge gained through his Italian studies, Rodin again employed drawing, using another special procedure. Judith Cladel related that, "having returned to Belgium, he executed a quantity of sketches, imposing on his models Michelangelesque poses."[65] Two sheets of life sketches in the Musée Rodin collection (*Figs. 23 and 24*) document this practice, with models in the poses of the *David*, both Louvre *Slaves*, *Dusk* from the Lorenzo de' Medici tomb, the *Christ* in Santa Maria Sopra Minerva, and the *Victory* of the Palazzo Vecchio (not all shown here). A curious gouached study in the Maryhill Museum, Maryhill, Washington, apparently dates from this same period, showing a pose derived from the Bargello *Apollo*, with the opposition of axes exaggerated (*Fig. 25*).

Taking the life studies of these poses, Rodin then traced them, in pen and sepia, onto sheets of thin paper, and elaborated them with draperies, accessories, and additional personages, to arrive at images of Bacchantes, Madonnas, and Icarus figures that appear to be ideas for sculpture. This procedure can be seen as the origin, if not of specific extant statues, then of a process of compositional thinking notable in much of Rodin's later sculptural work. In drawing, as later in sculpture, Rodin sought to multiply the usefulness of the figures he created. Thus, either by tracing or by a "carbon-copy" transfer process, he made repeated "casts" of his drawings, which he would then combine with tracings of other separately conceived figures and/or with direct elaborative additions, to produce new ensembles, such as Figure 26.[66] According to Cladel, six months after his return from Italy Rodin decided to work from postures taken naturally by his models.[67] However, such directly Michelangelesque sculptures as *Adam* and the man in the *Romeo and Juliet* ensemble indicate the period of Michelangelesque posing continued to provide inspiration; this is corroborated by the sequences of reworkings of the traced figures, and by related studies drawn beside them on their mount sheets.

His Italian trip was the spur that induced Rodin to undertake a reexamination and consolidation of his previous work. Evidence of such self-evaluation exists in a series of montage sheets at the Musée Rodin, put together by the artist. The support sheets show signs of having been bound together in an album, and many of them originally bore sanguine landscapes in the manner of Rodin's Belgian period.[68] They are now covered by a collection of miscellaneous drawings, ranging from early student works to drawings of the Italian trip and the post-Italian Michelangelesque period. Unfortunately, the subsequent dismantling of some of these sheets since Rodin's death, and apparently after primary cataloguing, makes it impossible to establish the proper rapport between many studies that were formerly side-by-side. From the montages that remain intact, it can be seen that Rodin brought together various drawings with an eye to an over-all compositional or thematic unity, and that he not only frequently reworked and retitled mounted drawings of all types (sometimes changing their nature entirely) but also redeveloped their themes in separate later sketches on the mount sheets themselves.[69] The drawings glued down indicate that the mounting could not have been done before 1875 and was probably done no later than 1880;[70] it is likely that the first consistent reworking of the Dantesque sheets also comes at this time.

Rodin's work at the Sèvres Porcelain Manufacture, in a full-blown eighteenth-century manner, more dramatically than ever demonstrates his ability to operate simultaneously in disparate modes. Rodin joined the special personnel of Sèvres in 1879, at the invitation of Carrier-Belleuse, who then presided as its director. The floral ambiance and infant type in studies from this year for the *Vase of the Elements* (*Fig. 27*) awake memories of Rodin's student days. However, in their handling, these and other infants connected with the Sèvres period display a moodier, more Prud'honesque shading than their predecessors, and seem to move in a nocturnal atmosphere of stomped shadow; this suggests not only Rodin's consideration of the relief effects of porcelain, but also the strong contrasts of contemporary gouache drawings.[71]

Figures 28 and 29 are also related to vase compositions (*Fig. 30*). Though later reworkings of both of the drawings complicate the matter, it seems that the initial drawings for the Sèvres pieces were characterized by fine-line execution that may well be the result of tracing,[72] and a system of shading based on tightly spaced, fine parallel diagonals that anticipate Rodin's drypoint manner of the early 1880's (*Fig. 44*).

Also in the general spirit and eighteenth-century mode of the Sèvres works is a series of large black chalk drawings (*Figs. 31, 32, and 33*) of light-suffused figural groups representing The Golden Age, Springtime, and Motherhood. Their manner is suggestive of Clodion, and also of Carrier-Belleuse.[73] However, these drawings bear no direct relation to Rodin's well-documented production during his sojourn at Sèvres. The inscription on Figure 33, describing it as a project for a marble statue in 1878, helps to establish a date for the group but adds to its curiosity, for the artist was not in the habit of preconceiving sculptural projects in this highly finished fashion.

The great majority of Rodin drawings that do relate directly to specific sculptures are not designs at all, in fact, but are studies of completed works, and the first of these known (*Fig. 34*), after the plaster of *The Age of Bronze*, dates to this same period; it was done in 1877 as an illustration for an article on the Salon in which the figure appeared.[74] Rodin's friend Roger Marx affirmed that such images of sculptures were the first Rodin drawings to come to public attention, and related that the sculptor did them to avoid the deformations he feared in photographic reproduction.[75] It was a common practice to have sculptors provide illustrative drawings, and there is, indeed, little of uncommon quality

28. *Embracing Couple*, c. 1880. Pencil, pen and ink, gouache. 6¼ x 3½ inches. Rodin Museum, Philadelphia Museum of Art. Given by Jules Mastbaum. *Actual size.*

29. *Couple with Putto,* c. 1880. Pen and ink. 7 x 5 inches. Rodin Museum, Philadelphia Museum of Art. Given by Jules Mastbaum.

30. *Two Vases,* c. 1880. Ceramic. Present location unknown.

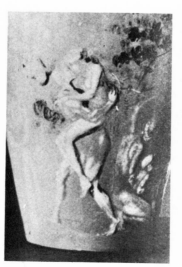

31. *The Golden Age (L'Age d'Or)*, c. 1878. Black chalk heightened with white. 18⁷⁄₁₆ x 12 inches. The Metropolitan Museum of Art, New York. Rogers Fund, 1963.

32. *Springtime (Le Printemps)*, c. 1878. Black
chalk. 17¼ x 11¼ inches. Collection of Mr. and
Mrs. Hugo Perls, New York.

33. *Young Mother Playing with Her Child (Jeune
mère jouant avec son enfant)*, 1878. Black chalk.
17¹¹⁄₁₆ x 11⅜ inches. Present location unknown.
Reproduced from *The Vasari Society*, Vol. III, No.
18, 1922.

34. *The Age of Bronze*, 1877. Pen and ink. 12⅜ x 9³⁄₁₆ inches. Cabinet des Dessins, Musée du Louvre, Paris.

35. *The Age of Bronze*, 1883. Pen and ink. Size and present location unknown. Reproduced from the *Gazette des Beaux-Arts*, December, 1833.

36. *St. John the Baptist*, 1880. Pen and ink. 12¹¹⁄₁₆ x 8¹³⁄₁₆ inches. Fogg Art Museum, Harvard University, Cambridge, Massachusetts. Bequest of Grenville L. Winthrop.

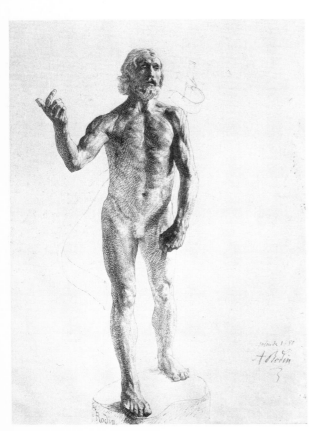

37. *St. John the Baptist* (detail of Figure 36).

38. *Centaur*, c. 1880. Sepia, ink, gouache over pencil. 5⅞ x 7⅞ inches. Musée des Beaux-Arts, Lyon.

39. *Dante*, c. 1880. Watercolor, ink, gouache.
6½ x 5½ inches. Rodin Museum, Philadelphia Museum of Art. Given by Jules Mastbaum.

40. *Ugolino*, c. 1880. Ink, gouache. 7⁹⁄₁₆ x
5⅞ inches. Musée Rodin, Paris (no. 5624).
Photograph by Bernès-Maroteau.

41. *Figure Studies (Etudes des figures)*, 1881. Drypoint etching, impression with plate canceled by the artist. 8¾ x 6¹⁵⁄₁₆ inches. Collection of Mr. and Mrs. Laurence Brunswick, Jr., Rydal, Pennsylvania.

42. *Shades Speaking to Dante*, c. 1880. Sepia, ink, gouache over pencil. 7⅝ x 4¹⁄₁₆ inches. Fogg Art Museum, Harvard University, Cambridge, Massachusetts. Bequest of Grenville L. Winthrop.

in this effort, which pales by comparison with its counterparts in the next decade.[76]

If we compare the 1877 drawing, for example, with another work after *The Age of Bronze*, published in 1883, (*Fig. 35*), we can see an enormous advance in Rodin's abilities. In an approach that, hardly coincidentally, resembles that of the modeling of *The Age of Bronze* sculpture, the earlier work painstakingly renders all the details of modeling. The technique is a rather undistinguished variety of loose hatching, which fails to convey a potent sense of volume.

The 1883 version, on the other hand, seems to reflect the broader modeling of *The Gates of Hell* figures and displays a far more confident and effective draftsmanship. The artist's use of light in this later drawing is reminiscent of his practice of studying sculpture by candlelight.[77] The highlights and an insistently clear and continuous outline stress the exterior silhouette; the mesh of free hatchwork within serves to suggest modeling and at the same time lends the whole a unity and weight not present in the earlier attempt. The technique of active cross-hatching to define volumes can be found in the works of other sculptors, as shown in the illustrated Salon catalogues of the time; however, other artists tended to use *hachures* only to establish shaded areas, and their drawings are much lighter and less dense than those of Rodin, who used the dark web of hatching to suggest the bronze surface, inversely employing a minimum of blank paper to render volume by highlights.[78]

Rodin's statue of *St. John the Baptist*, which appeared in the Salon of 1880, is the subject of what is perhaps the finest drawing after sculpture in this mode (*Fig. 36*). A detail of the study (*Fig. 37*) helps to clarify Rodin's procedure: Over a base of summary indications in light pencil, the dark surfaces are built up in layers of spiky omnidirectional pen hatching, with increasingly dark solutions of ink; modeling in lighted areas is suggested by clusters of short flecked strokes or dots. The end result is a forceful blend of energy and solidity, conveying both the modulations of volume and the varied effects of light on the surface.

Though Rodin could have seen expressive *hachure* work in Michelangelo's drawings in 1875,[79] or, earlier, in those of Carpeaux, Delacroix, or Géricault, he did not develop the mode personally until after 1877. It became a characteristic style in the 1880's, undergoing modification in the direction of thinner layering and looser play of line. A clear command of the process, however, was already established by 1880, when the *St. John* was published.[80]

1880–90

In the 1880's, Rodin was occupied by work on several major monuments, beginning with *The Gates of Hell* in 1880, and including *The Burghers of Calais* (1884), and the *Monument to Victor Hugo* (1886). Though the sculpture of this period moved toward an increasingly direct, unallegorical approach to the body, the "black" gouached sheets traditionally assigned to the 1880's deal exclusively with literary or mythological and imaginative themes (*Figs. 18, 38, 39, and 40*). As mentioned before, these latter drawings have been held to represent Rodin's thinking in the development of *The Gates of Hell*. Yet only one or two such drawings known offer a close enough correspondence to figures in *The Gates* to be considered source projects.[81] Both anomalies are understandable when we realize that the gouached imaginative researches in fact declined very sharply after the early 1880's, if they continued at all.

The most valuable published source for Rodin's "black" drawings is *Les Dessins d'Auguste Rodin*, 142 facsimiles produced by the Maison Goupil in 1897. This collection presents a comprehensive diversity of imaginative subjects and styles (*Figs. 16, 38, 39, 42, and 65*). In an interview of 1900, discussing his work on *The Gates*, Rodin specifically dated these drawings. He said, "I lived a whole year with Dante, . . . drawing the eight circles of his Hell." When the interviewer asked, "And these drawings constituted the genesis of your work?" the artist replied, "No, at the end of a year, I saw that these drawings, if they rendered my vision of Dante, were not close enough to reality. And I started all over, after Nature, working with my models. . . . I had abandoned my drawings after Dante. One of my friends . . . had them reproduced . . . by the Maison Goupil."[82]

As suggested before, Rodin "mined" his collected drawings to provide the basis for these new efforts. So many of the images in the Goupil volume result from the kind of reworking evident in the two-layer construction of Figure 39 that an attempt to distinguish drawings done wholly in 1880–81 is risky at best. The few drawings definitely datable to the period, several architectural projects for *The Gates*[83] and one drypoint (*Fig. 41*),[84] show the figural and compositional characteristics of the earlier "Dantesque" works, rendered with a greater decisiveness of line. In the case of the drypoint, as well as in the reworking of another drawing connected with *The Gates* (*Fig. 42*), the blank faces and summary line conventions of the early "Dantesque" images are replaced by detailed grotesqueness of features, perhaps reflecting the artist's desire for greater specificity of visualization in the face of a definite commission.

In any case, whether totally original or the product of reworking, Goupil figures like the *Centaur* (*Fig. 38*) clearly represent the full development of the gouached imaginative style; a blend of dark and light gouaches and sepia conveys strong, dense volumes and dramatic light, while outlines are rendered in bold pen strokes of high continuity.[85] Yet it can be proved that this drawing was completed at the latest in 1883, when it was published, along with Figure 42, in *L'Art*.[86]

Though this evidence is consistent with Rodin's statement that he "abandoned" the drawings from Dante early in the decade, it can be argued that the "black" style cannot be considered terminated at that time. The artist continued to use gouache and ink washes in his drawings of Victor Hugo in 1883 (*Fig. 49*) and in works done as late as 1888. Furthermore, the fact that plate No. 34 in the Goupil publication, Figure 15, and others like them in the Musée Rodin bear the written comment "Victor Hugo" or simply "Hugo" attests to the artist's return to these works in the late 1880's in connection with the project for the *Monument to Victor Hugo* (which was commissioned in 1886). The written comments on these and other drawings (*Fig. 42*) certainly confirm that the sheets were intended by Rodin solely for his own use.[87] In this sense, such drawings were only finished when they left his possession; as long as they were available to him, in this decade and the early part of the next, they remained a viable source of reference. Nonetheless, the slight reworkings that accompany "Hugo" notations suggest that such reconsideration, after about 1881–82, did not result in changes in essential images or style, and need not contradict a chronological assignation to the beginning of the decade.[88]

If Rodin turned in 1881 from traditional imaginative sources to direct work with his models, as not only his statement but also the unorthodox poses of sculptural studies of the 1880's indicate he did, we have no known drawings to document the change. None of the gouached drawings indicate a live model. The void prompts the conclusion that Rodin's draftsmanship was in a state of stasis in the later 1880's, not responding to the innovations he undertook in sculpture.

In terms of intrinsic quality, though, some of Rodin's most admirable graphic work dates from this period: a series of drypoint prints.[89] Rodin learned the technique in 1881 from his friend Alphonse Legros. His first attempt, *Love Turning the World* (*Les Amours conduisant le monde*), is already quite accomplished (*Fig. 43*). No direct source for the print is known, but the connection with the contemporary work at Sèvres is unmistakable.[90] The execution in 1881 of both this print and the "Dantesque" *Figure Studies* (*Etudes*) (*Fig. 41*) presents a stylistic dichotomy repeated two years later with the appearance of both *Springtime* (*Le Printemps*) (*Fig. 44*) and *The Circle* (*La Ronde*) (*Fig. 45*). The latter two, in turn, form with the *Bellone* (a female personification of war) of the same year (*Fig. 46*) an important three-point statement of Rodin's draftsmanship in this period. In *The Circle*, as in *Figure Studies* of 1881, the more pessimistic and arcane side of Rodin's imagination takes its characteristically aggressive, grotesque form;[91] while *Springtime*, like *Love Turning the World*, casts a lyrical theme in the smoother eighteenth-century manner (*Springtime* corresponds to a plaque and vase made for Sèvres).[92] Since none of these works was specifically commissioned, or intended for exhibition or sale,[93] the ensemble suggests that the mode of *Springtime* and *Love Turning the World* cannot be dismissed as retrograde or merely commercial, but must be considered as representative of lighter, more optimistic strains as much a part of the artist's psyche as the more sinister "Dantesque" visions.

The third 1883 print, *Bellone*, would more properly be called *Portrait of Madame Rodin*, as Rodin himself so entitled it in one dedication.[94] A comparison with the late 1870's sculpture of *Bellone*, for which Rose Beuret also posed, will show that the drypoint does not re-create the sculpture's bellicose snarl. The print is instead a true portrait, in which the pretentious costume and girlish hair offset an uncompromisingly frank presentation of the blunted, melancholy beauty of Rose at thirty-nine. Though the print may at first seem technically timid, the contrast of the loose, playful lines of hair and helmet with the solid parallel shading of the pensive face provides a moving image. With *Springtime* and *The Circle* of the same year, *Bellone* offers proof of the artist's ability to change his graphic approach to conform to his observation of life and to the disparate poles of his imagination.

The apogee of Rodin's drypoint production, and of his graphic portraiture, came in 1884, in the *Victor Hugo in Three-Quarters View* (*Figs. 47 and 48*). In 1883, Rodin had made quick sketches, from all angles, of the writer's head, in preparation for a sculpted bust (*Fig. 49*);[95] Hugo had refused formal sittings. From these sketches, now lost, and from memory, Rodin produced the bust of Victor Hugo as well as two drypoints: Figure 47 and a less successful *Victor Hugo Full Face*, in 1886.

In the former, Rodin's characteristic disinclination to remove the marks of his preliminary work has left a two-part demonstration of his elements of facture (*Fig. 48*). At the left the "ghost" of a first attempt shows the care taken to establish, in dotted lines, the essential points of the form;[96] while on the right, a jagged storm of interweaving strokes, accented by flecks, slashes, and gouges, caricatures the leonine energy of Hugo's personality.

In the final three-quarters view of Hugo, as in the *St. John*, of 1880, energy and control merge; but in the portrait, the balance is tipped toward energy, and the image depends less on a consistent *hachure* than on a variety of suggestive effects produced by lines of increased individual freedom. Rodin insists on the clarity of the forehead silhouette, and renders the eyes in a rich, solid black. Using these and the more densely modeled cheeks as the bearers of resemblance, he loosens the mesh of strokes as he moves out, leaving the upper face a stable outcropping in a tossing sea of linear energy.

Rodin's further essays in this manner did not maintain this balance between spontaneity and structural justness. In the triple portrait of *Henri Becque* (*Fig. 50*), for example, the modeling is more erratic, and the loosening of hatching results in a cobweb that sacrifices structural potency for atmospheric effects. This developing atmospheric concern

43. *Love Turning the World (Les Amours conduisant le monde)*, 1881. Drypoint etching. 7⅞ x 9⅞ inches. National Gallery of Art, Washington, D.C. Gift of Mrs. John W. Simpson.

44. *Springtime (Le Printemps)*, 1883. Drypoint etching. 5⅞ x 3¹⁵⁄₁₆ inches. Courtesy, Museum of Fine Arts, Boston. Gift of Mr. and Mrs. Peter A. Wick.

45. *The Circle (La Ronde)*, 1883. Drypoint etching. 9¹⁄₁₆ x 7 inches. Bibliothèque Nationale, Paris.

46. *Bellone*, 1883. Drypoint etching. 5⅞ x 3¹⁵⁄₁₆ inches. National Gallery of Art, Washington, D.C. Gift of Mrs. John W. Simpson.

47. *Victor Hugo in Three-Quarters View*, 1884. Drypoint etching. 8¾ x 6¹⁵⁄₁₆ inches. National Gallery of Art, Washington, D.C.

48. *Victor Hugo in Three-Quarters View* (detail of Figure 47).

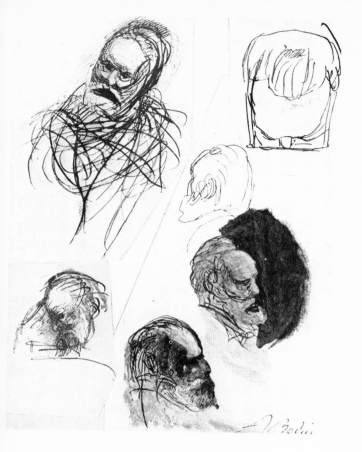

49. *Studies of the Head of Victor Hugo,*
1883. Pen and ink, gouache. Size and present location unknown.

50. *Henri Becque,* 1885. Drypoint etching.
6¼ x 8 inches. National Gallery of Art,
Washington, D.C.

was more successfully realized three years later in a series of pen drawings among Rodin's 1888 illustrations for Baudelaire's *Les Fleurs du
Mal*.[97]

Six of the twenty-five illustrations are based directly on sculpture
(*Figs. 51 and 52*).[98] In these six, the surface of the figures show a hatching system like that in the *Henri Becque*; outside the bodies, though, the
line system gives way to disconnected fantasies, in more slack, curving
pen motions. The environment created suggests a distinct change in
Rodin's vision of his own sculpture; compare, for example, the hazy
chiaroscuro of the torso of *Meditation* in Figure 51 with the sculpture
drawings of the early 1880's (*Figs. 35 and 36*). This change is also noticeable in the washed rendering of the bust of *Madame Vicuña*, also done
in 1888 (*Fig. 53*).

The "black" style appears in three of the Baudelaire illustrations.
At least one of these (*Fig. 54*) is directly traceable to previous drawings,[99] and, as the images bear only very indirect, if any, reference to the
poems they accompany, it seems likely that all three were taken from
previous gouached studies. This would make them comparable in origin
to the illustrations based on sculpture, as well as to many line drawings
in the series, which can be directly linked to other "Dantesque" drawings.[100]

Investigations of Rodin's imaginative drawings suggest, in fact, that
very few of the Baudelaire illustrations were invented specifically for
this purpose.[101] This accords with Rodin's practice as an illustrator;
when confronted with a commission, he frequently searched the art he
had already produced for figures to fit the context at hand. We have
already remarked this procedure in the drawings related to *The Gates*,
and in those that bear notations for the *Monument to Victor Hugo*; it
is even more apparent in Rodin's illustrations for Emile Bergerat's
Enguerrande (Paris: Frinzine and Klein, 1884).

In these two drawings (*Figs. 55 and 56*) Rodin adapted pieces of
sculpture, *Eve* and a figure from the lower left of *The Gates* (just below
Ugolino), to the context of the poem.[102] Narrative is thus combined
uneasily with an attitude more particular to Rodin: the idea that his
works bore such a host of symbolic resonances that they could serve
again and again in different combinations and contexts. When later
drawings were inserted into such texts as Octave Mirbeau's *Le Jardin
des Supplices* and Ovid's *Elégies Amoreuses*, they were not adapted at
all, and correspondences were left to the reader's imagination.[103]

As Albert Elsen has remarked, the frontispiece (*Fig. 57*) and other
drawings like it among the Baudelaire illustrations display a new economy of means in Rodin's work.[104] The pure linear style probably derives
from such tracings of previous gouached work as *Group of Figures* (*Fig.
58*),[105] and points toward Rodin's drawings of the 1890's.

The Baudelaire illustrations as a whole, though, are a fitting summation of the drawings of the 1880's. The pages review the graphic styles of the decade, in confident, personalized draftsmanship. Moreover, it is symptomatic that the quality of their handling is not accompanied by a comparable originality of motifs. In the case of the Baudelaire drawings, the phenomenon may be attributed to Rodin's self-confessed lack of time and incentive during their execution.[106] But, from the drawings for *The Gates*, through *Springtime* and *The Circle*, to the Bergerat illustrations, and finally to these Baudelaire pages, Rodin's 1880's draftsmanship developed within a pattern of reworking previously conceived motifs; even the *Bellone* involved an older sculptural format.

Some of the more spontaneous work of the 1880's, like the Victor Hugo drawings, may be lost or as yet unstudied. It seems clear, though, that drawings did not play a crucial role in Rodin's development in these years. Previously, in his student years and again in the 1860's and 1870's, Rodin brought drawing study to bear on his sculpture; in the following decade, the situation was reversed. Rodin, in writing of his later drawings to the sculptor Antoine Bourdelle, after 1900, summarized it succinctly: "My drawings," he said, "are the result of my sculpture."[107]

1890–1900

It has often been held that Rodin drew very little in the 1890's. The line of reasoning was expressed by one scholar as follows:

> Around 1890, Rodin was so absorbed by his numerous and mammoth sculptural projects that he no longer had the time to give to drawing. . . . it was only after the beginning of the century that he returned to this exercise, which was doubtless at the same time a rest and a stimulant for him. . . . [the] drawings of the dancers, especially the female dancers of Cambodia [in 1906] came to form the beginning of a second period of apogee in Rodin's drawings, the period which—by opposition to that of the gouached drawings of around 1880— could be called 'the period of the watercolor drawings.'[108]

This account, however, is not accurate. Rodin's later drawing mode was not simply a diversion of the aging artist, but rather an offspring of the same energies which produced his most innovative major sculpture, the *Monument to Balzac*, in 1890–98. More than a change in style, the later drawings represent a new approach to the act of drawing, as described by the writer Clément Janin in 1903 (*Figs. 59, 60, 61 and 76*).

In his recent drawings, Rodin uses nothing more than a contour heightened with a wash. Here is how he goes about it.

51 and 52. Illustrations for Charles Baudelaire's *La Beauté* and *Le Guignon*, 1888.
Pen and ink. 6⅞ x 4⅜ inches. Musée Rodin, Paris.

Les poëtes devant mes grandes attitudes,
Qu'on dirait que j'emprunte aux plus fiers monuments,
Consumeront leurs jours en d'austères études ;

Car j'ai pour fasciner ces dociles amants
De purs miroirs qui font les étoiles plus belles :
Mes yeux, mes larges yeux aux clartés éternelles !

— Maint joyau dort enseveli
Dans les ténébres et l'oubli,
Bien loin des pioches et des sondes ;

Mainte fleur épanche à regret
Son parfum doux comme un secret
Dans les solitudes profondes.

53. *Bust of Mme. Vicuña,* 1888. Pen and ink, sepia, gouache. 6⁵⁄₁₆ x 4¼ inches. Cabinet des Dessins, Musée du Louvre.

54. Illustration for Charles Baudelaire's *De Profundis Clamavi,* 1888. Pen and ink, watercolor, gouache. 6⅞ x 4⅜ inches. Musée Rodin, Paris.

55. Illustration for Emile Bergerat's *Enguerrande*, 1884. Pen and ink (?). 11 x 8¼ inches. Bibliothèque National-ale, Paris.

56. Illustration for Emile Bergerat's *Enguerrande*, 1884. Pen and ink (?). 11 x 8¼ inches. Bibliothèque Nationale, Paris.

57. Frontispiece for Charles Baudelaire's *Fleurs du Mal*, 1888. Pen and ink, 4¼ x 6⁵⁄₁₆ inches. Musée Rodin, Paris. *Actual size.*

58. *Group of Figures (Le Temps)*, c. 1885–90. Pen and ink, gouache. 4⅞ x 4¹³⁄₁₆ inches. Collection of Mr. and Mrs. Laurence Brunswick, Jr., Rydal, Pennsylvania.

59. *Standing Female Nude, Arms Raised*, c. 1900. Pen and ink, watercolor wash. 12 x 7½ inches. Collection of Mrs. Jefferson Dickson, Beverly Hills. On indefinite loan to the Yale University Art Gallery.

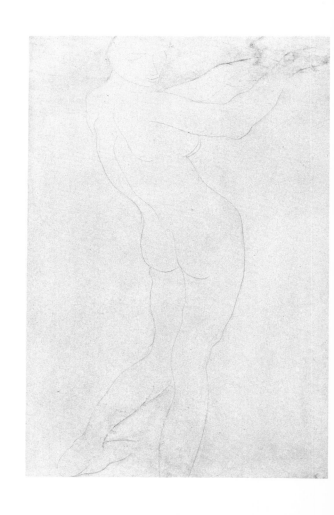

60. *Standing Nude*, c. 1900. Pencil, watercolor wash. 12¾ x 8½ inches. The Montreal Museum of Fine Arts. The F. Cleveland Morgan Collection, 1962.

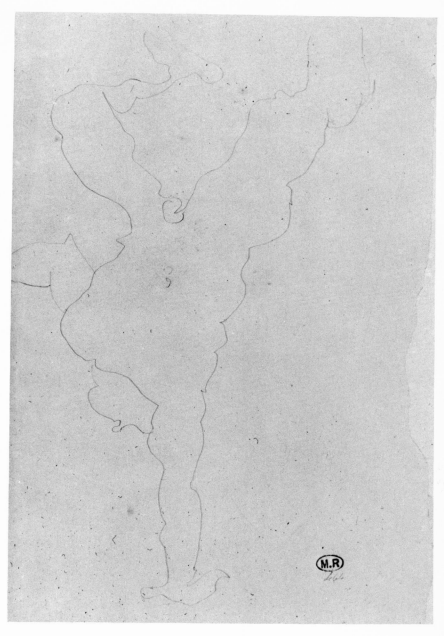

61. *Nude Male Standing on One Hand*, c. 1900. Lead pencil. 12¼ x 7¾ inches. Musée Rodin, Paris (no. 464). Photograph by Adelys.

Equipped with a sheet of ordinary paper posed on a board, and with a lead pencil—sometimes a pen—he has his model take an essentially unstable pose, then he draws spiritedly, without taking his eyes off the model. The hand goes where it will: often the pencil falls off the page; the drawing is thus decapitated or loses a limb by amputation. . . . The master has not looked at it once. In less than a minute, this snapshot of movement is caught. It contains, naturally, some excessive deformations, unforeseen swellings, but, if the relation of proportions is destroyed, on the other hand, each section has its contours and the cursive, schematic indication at its modeling. The correction lines are numerous. Often the pencil, in the swiftness of its progress, misses the contour of a breast, the flex of a thigh; Rodin then goes back over this part with hasty strokes which mix together, but in which the just line is found.

This first effort completed, Rodin takes up the work again, sometimes corrects it directly with a stroke of red pencil; but most often, it is in tracing that he rectifies it. His great preoccupation at this time is to conserve and even to amplify the impression of life that he has obtained from the direct sketch. . . . According to him, his secret for fixing the form in the atmosphere is to enlarge it, to give it five quarters instead of four. The tone that he adds, this wash of Sienna which goes over the limits of the line, seems capricious or negligent, and has, in reality, the effect of thickening this enlargement, as well as binding together the contours.[109]

Drawings of this type were exhibited by Rodin in his special pavilion at the Universal Exposition of 1900,[110] and were both described and reproduced in periodicals of that year (*Fig. 62*).[111] Moreover, such drawings had been exhibited in Brussels in May, 1899.[112] In recounting visits with Rodin in 1898, Judith Cladel characterizes the late aquarelles precisely, and describes them as numerous;[113] her accounts are supported by the description of another writer, published in August of 1898.[114] Furthermore, such drawings were reproduced as early as 1897.[115]

The most convincing date for the origin of this new mode was given by Rodin's friend, the critic Roger Marx, in *L'Image* of September, 1897. Marx here remarked "a series of drawings, an undertaking no longer dependent on convention, but with the model, around the summer of 1896"; in context, the reference is unquestionably to Rodin's late aquarelles.[116]

Though Marx suggests that this series sprang more or less full-blown into life, it seems likely that some transitional work preceded it. The small sketches that may link the late 1880's to the mid-1890's are exemplified by Figure 63; these nymphets have a pure linearity that prefigures later contour handling, yet they retain traditional poses and wholly conventional anatomy. The mood of these figure studies, as well as many of the transitional stylistic features, can be seen in the drypoint published as a frontispiece to Gustave Geffroy's *La Vie Artistique*, of 1893 (*Fig. 64*).[117] Though the violence and dramatic effects of the imaginative drawings of the 1880's have abated, the body type, facial conventions, and poses of these *Souls in Purgatory* relate closely to drawings such as *Castor and Pollux* (*Fig. 65*), which figured in the Goupil ensemble. We may hypothesize that, during the first half of the 1890's, figures of this type began to display foreshortened limbs and less restricted movement, incorporating the observation of live models, as in the *Dancing Figures* (*Fig. 66*), which was probably executed around 1894–95.

Another drawing probably of about 1895, and published in 1899 as a frontispiece for Octave Mirbeau's *Le Jardin des Supplices*, clearly indicates a live model (*Fig. 67*). Yet a comparison with an aquarelle used to illustrate a 1902 edition of the same poems (*Fig. 68*) shows that the 1899 frontispiece retains conventional anatomical traits similar to both the nymphet of Figure 63 and to some of the Baudelaire illustrations of 1888: an adolescent, small-breasted body with thin extremities and long lower quarters with hips that do not suggest the muscular and skeletal interactions of the pelvis. The life drawing in Figure 69 may represent the penultimate stage of this development, for, though it shows the line continuity and response to anatomy of the later manner, its small format, paper type, and wash mixed gouache suggest lingering habits of previous work.

As the 1893 frontispiece is our only secure document in the 1890–96 period, and as it reproduces a drawing of indeterminate date,[118] the reader is cautioned not to believe that our developmental hypothesis precludes the possibility of drawings in other manners in this period.[119] For example, Rodin produced such portrait renderings as that of the lady novelist Séverine (*Fig. 70*), of 1893; the whipped activity of its free charcoal strokes over a base of stomped modeling derives ultimately from the early *académies*. A similarly impressive charcoal of Octave Mirbeau (*Fig. 71*), probably from the later part of the decade, shows a more restrained stroking and greater breadth of treatment that contrast not only with the *Séverine* but most especially with the pen study of Mirbeau done by Rodin in 1892 (*Fig. 72*). This latter was apparently one of many drawings with which Rodin decorated books for his friends.[120]

If such drawings do provide continuity in the 1890's, the major form of Rodin's graphic expression, the figure study, underwent a change that seems bewilderingly complete. When we compare the gouached drawings of the 1880's with such works as Figures 61, 68, and 75, it is difficult to decipher a consistent development. However, just as the works of the early 1880's represented the definitive fusion of previous ideas, so these later drawings and aquarelles were the culmination of concepts long

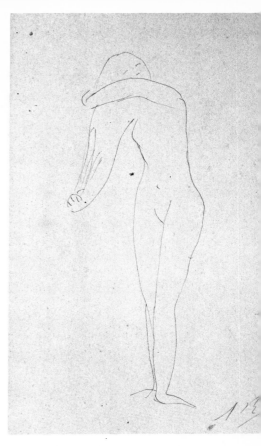

62. Line drawings, before 1900. Lead pencil (?). Reproduced from *La Revue Blanche*, June 15, 1900.

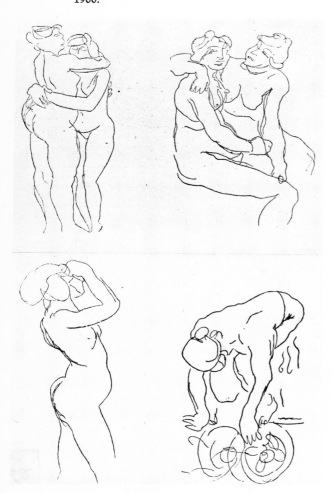

63. *Standing Nude Figure*, c. 1890. Pen and ink. 6¾ x 4³⁄₁₆ inches. Yale University Art Gallery, New Haven. The Jules E. Mastbaum Collection. Gift of his daugther, Mrs. Jefferson Dickson.

64. *Souls in Purgatory (Ames du Purgatoire),* 1893. Frontispiece for Gustave Geffroy's *La Vie Artistique.* Drypoint etching. 6¹⁄₁₆ x 3⅞ inches. Bibliothèque Nationale, Paris.

65. *Castor and Pollux (La Seine),* c. 1885–90. Pen and ink, watercolor wash. 5⅛ x 4⅛ inches. Rodin Museum, Philadelphia Museum of Art. Gift of Jules Mastbaum.

66. *Dancing Figures*, c. 1894–95. Pen and ink, lead pencil. 9 x 7¼ inches. Collection of Mr. and Mrs. Laurence Brunswick, Jr., Rydal, Pennsylvania.

67. Frontispiece for Octave Mirbeau's *Le Jardin des Supplices* (Paris, 1899), c. 1895–96. Bibliothèque Nationale, Paris.

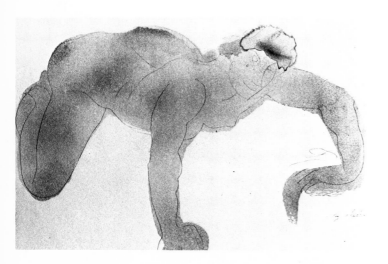

68. Illustration for Octave Mirbeau's *Le Jardin des Supplices* (Paris, 1902), c. 1898–99. Color lithograph. 12⅞ x 9¹⁵⁄₁₆ inches. Rodin Museum, Philadelphia Museum of Art.

69. *Standing Nude Combing Hair,* c. 1895–96. Lead pencil, watercolor wash. 8¾₁₆ x 4¹¹⁄₁₆ inches. Yale University Art Gallery, New Haven. Gift of Mrs. Jefferson Dickson. *Actual size.*

70. *Séverine*, c. 1893. Charcoal. 12⅝ x 10⅝ inches. Budapest Museum of Art.

71. *Octave Mirbeau*, c. 1900. Charcoal. 18¼ x
17¼ inches. Roland, Browse, & Delbanco, London.

72. *Octave Mirbeau*, 1892. Pen and ink. Size and
present location unknown.

present in the artist's mind. Rodin traced their point of departure, in fact, to 1875. "Michelangelo," he wrote to Bourdelle after 1900,

> gave me some invaluable perceptions, and I copied him in my spirit, in certain of my works, before understanding him. Once I understood, I saw that this movement [I had seen in his figures] existed in nature, and that I had only to avoid losing that in my models. . . . that this movement was something natural, not something I could impose artificially; from that point originate my drawings, which came a long time afterwards, however, and in which one will find Michelangelo again, in such a natural form that one will not suspect it.[121]

In the late 1870's, in response to his new understanding of movement, Rodin opened two paths that eventually led to his later drawings. First, he began to study from models moving freely in his studio—a practice that brings to mind the special training of Lecoq.[122] Second, in order to introduce natural movement into art, he developed the idea of expressing in one work both the beginning and the result of a motion. Essayed first in the stride of the statue of *St. John the Baptist* (1878–79), this concept was a factor in the rapidity of the late life drawings, as Rodin explained to H. E. C. Dujardin-Beaumetz: "The sketch allows the movement more nearly to approach the action. In order to express a movement in all its character and truth, it is important that it be at once the result of successive movements which have preceded the moment of fixity, and that it foreshadow the sensations of the movements which follow."[123] If we could see the quick sketches Rodin made of Javanese dancers at the 1889–90 Universal Exposition, or those done before that of Japanese dancers, they might show how Rodin's drafting style adjusted to this interest prior to the 1890's; however, no sheets have been convincingly attached to either of these series, and Figure 66 seems to be our earliest glimpse of such study.[124]

Rodin's later life-drawings, like the early studies that probed the structure of the Medici tomb figures, were a means to test his knowledge, his command. In the studies of 1875, however, structures were conceived and imposed by the artist. At the initial level of the later life-drawings, Rodin sought to register, almost seismographically, rather than to invent. Lecoq trained Rodin to draw the figure without looking at it, from memory. Strengthened by a lifetime of study of the body, Rodin carried this instruction to an unforeseen conclusion, by exactly reversing its mechanics, never taking his eyes off the model, never looking at the paper. The primary life-drawing of Rodin's later manner is not the conscious creation of a shape resembling a static object in nature, but a record of a perception of form in transition, in which the verisimilitude of the shape created is subservient to an emphasis on the act, rather than the result, of drawing. Rodin explained this to Antony Ludovici around 1906:

> Don't you see that, for my work of modeling, I have not only to possess a complete *knowledge* of the human form, but also a deep *feeling* for every aspect of it? I have, as it were, to *incorporate* the lines of the human body, and they must become part of myself, deeply seated in my instincts. I must feel them at the end of my fingers. All this must flow naturally from my eye to my hand. Only then can I be certain that I understand. Now look! What is this drawing? Not once in describing the shape of that mass did I shift my eyes from the model. Why? Because I wanted to be sure that nothing evaded my grasp of it. Not a thought about the technical problem of representing it on paper could be allowed to arrest the flow of my feelings about it, from my eye to my hand. The moment I drop my eyes that flow stops. That is why my drawings are only my way of testing myself. They are my way of proving to myself how far this incorporation of the subtle secrets of the human form has taken place within me. I try to see the figure as a mass, as volume. . . . Occasionally I get effects that are quite interesting, positions that are suggestive and stimulating; but that is by the way. My object is to test to what extent my hands already feel what my eyes see.[125]

Rodin challenged himself by attempting poses previously unknown in the history of art. Other artists of the nineteenth century, notably Delacroix, whose drawings Rodin admired,[126] produced drawings of great freedom and calligraphic intensity. However, none risked such daring poses or their resultant distortions (*Fig. 73*), and none achieved the blend of complexity and simplification seen in the single unbroken body contour of Figure 61.

Life-drawing was, however, only the first step of Rodin's work in the later manner; his practice of reworking and reapplying his drawings is seen once again in the post-1896 production. As Clément Janin described, the artist sometimes made corrections directly on the life-drawings, or washed them directly with watercolor. Most frequently, however, he would take a life-drawing such as Figure 59, hold it up to the window, place another sheet over it, and trace a second version (*Fig. 60*).[127] The traced version stabilizes the position on the page, reduces the distortions and *pentimenti*, and arrives at a more unified visual image. A great many of Rodin's late watercolor drawings, such as the dancing figure in The Art Institute of Chicago (*Fig. 74*), are undoubtedly the result of such distillations.

In this two-stage attempt to reconcile the particularities and energies of the active human form (in the life-drawings) with the desire for a more generalized, unified art (the tracings), Rodin's late drawings are connected with the development of *Balzac*. In making the monument, Rodin first expended every effort to inform himself on Balzac's appearance, making studies from figures and faces he felt resembled the deceased writer. But, having assimilated this life study, he went beyond it; the final form of the cloaked *Balzac*, arrived at in the same period as the late drawing manner, was a synthesis determined by considerations of the work of art as separate creation, summarizing and unifying the previous researches. "My principle," Rodin said of *Balzac*, "is to imitate not only form but also life. I search in nature for this life and amplify it by exaggerating the holes and the lumps. . . . after which I search for the synthesis of the whole."[128] The two steps are similar in the drawings, where the watercolor wash becomes, in a sense, the cloak of Balzac.

Line and wash as conceived in the late manner correspond to sculptural concepts of silhouette (or contour) and value, worked out by the artist in the *Balzac* project. The conception of the mode thus corresponded exactly to the goals of the sculptor's aesthetic as he explained it to Camille Mauclair in 1898. The goal of his sculpture, as Mauclair recorded his explanation, was

> . . . to obtain above all a *drawing of movement in the air*. It was to obey the natural principles of sculpture made to be seen in the open air, that is, the search for contour and for what the painters call *value*. In order to understand this notion exactly, one should think about what one sees of a person stood up against the light of the twilight sky: a very precise silhouette, filled by a dark coloration, with indistinct details. The rapport between this dark coloration and the tone of the sky is the value, that is to say, that which gives the notion of material substance to the body. . . . All that we see essentially of a statue standing high in place, and all that carries, is its movement, its contour, and its value.

Furthermore, the idea of "seismographic" rapid life-drawing leading to a reduction to simplified line and wash (through the tracings) is implicit in this same article.

> In sacrificing everything to the *drawing of movement*, Rodin held to a preoccupation with pure realism, for he [first] intensively studied the instinctive thrust of the personage, without thinking in advance of stylizing it.
>
> This double tendency, synthesization of the figure in reducing it to its silhouette and to its value, with a rapid and simultaneous study of movement in all its aspects, Rodin has felt growing in him over the years.

"The artist," remarked Mauclair at the end of the article, "in order to stress what he has said, showed me [along with several sculptures] some drawings with a single line, washed with a light watercolor, and synthesizing rapid movements."[129]

1900–1917

It may be helpful at this point to suggest a manner of classifying Rodin's late drawings. We may think of them as three basic types.

Type I, illustrated in Figures 59, 61, 75 and 76, is essentially a contour life drawing, done without looking at the page. Such drawings appear both with and without watercolor wash, but more frequently without. Even with a wash and/or stomping, the drawings retain the evidence of the initial rapid sketch; reworking lines may temper original distortions, but the highly continuous and more erratic initial strokes are evident. The great majority of Type I drawings are on a lightweight, smooth, wove paper, white or light cream in tone, with a fine mechanical surface tooth; the sheets are usually 12 to 12¼ inches tall by 7¾ to 8 inches wide.[130]

Type II drawings (*Figs. 77, 78, and 79*) are much more simplified in their contours; *pentimenti* are reduced if not eliminated, the proportions and position of the figure are stabilized, and most of the multiple smaller swerving movements of the Type I contour line are smoothed out. Whereas the Type I contour line shows a wide variety of densities and pencil pressures, the Type II line is more even.

In the large majority of cases, Type II drawings are found with watercolor wash. In fact, though the initial line work of a Type II sheet is simpler, the final facture is likely to be more complex than that of Type I, as Type II watercolors are more likely to have both a background wash and/or heavy reworking in wash and pencil.[131] The *Nero* of Figure 94 illustrates this point; the fine regularity of the original lines, visible in the stomach and left hand, mark this as a Type II work, but they are almost totally covered by added gouaches and pencil stroking. The blunted strokes at the bottom of the *Nero* are characteristic of Rodin's later additions to such works; they may also be seen in the drapery added to the Type II *Nude with Draperies* (*Fig. 74*). Also characteristic of Rodin's second- or third-level reworking are the thick, sweeping strokes that redefine the exterior silhouette of *Nero;* one or two such lines will often accent the major contours of an otherwise unretouched watercolor.

Type II sheets are distinguished from Type I by paper as well: a heavier, more resistant, wove paper, slightly rougher in surface and tending to be larger in size, commonly about 12¾ by 9¾ inches, but as large as 20 by 13 inches, in some cases. The same pose often occurs in both Type I and Type II drawings (*Figs. 59 and 60; Figs. 76 and 77*); in direct comparisons, this has proved to be almost certainly the result of tracing. The evidence of our research suggests that the greater part of all Type

73. *Reclining Nude*, c. 1900. Lead pencil. 7 x 11⁵⁄₁₆ inches. Collection of Mr. Claude Cueto, Paris.

74. *Nude with Draperies*, c. 1900–1905. Lead pencil, watercolor wash. 17½ x 12⅜ inches. Courtesy of The Art Institute of Chicago.

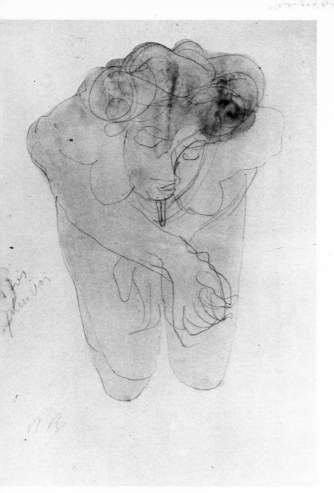

75. *Woman Kneeling, Front View*, before 1900. Lead pencil, watercolor wash. 11½ x 7½ inches. The Stanford Museum of Art, Stanford, California. Gift of Charles Feingarten.

76. *Dancing Figure*, c. 1900–1905. Lead pencil. 12⅜ x 8⁵⁄₁₆ inches. Musée Rodin, Paris (no. 2829). Photograph by Adelys.

77. *Dancing Figure*, before 1908. Lead pencil, watercolor wash. 12³⁄₁₆ x 9³⁄₄ inches.
National Gallery of Art, Washington, D.C. Gift of Mrs. John W. Simpson.

78. *Crouching Nude*, before 1900. Lead pencil, watercolor wash. 9½ x 12 inches.
Rodin Museum, Philadelphia Museum of Art. Given by Jules Mastbaum.

79. *Crouching Nude*, c. 1900–1905. Lead pencil, watercolor wash. 8¾ x 12¹³⁄₁₆ inches.
The Stanford Museum of Art, Stanford, California. Gift of B. G. Cantor Foundation.

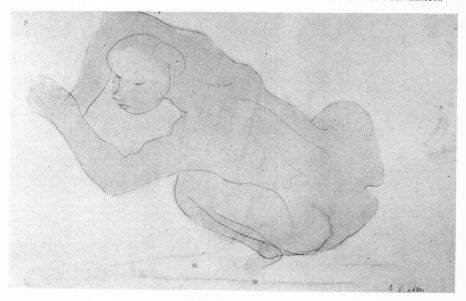

II drawings is the product of tracing, and all such drawings can be seen as representing some form of distillation from separate life-studies. Some shapes, such as the kneeling vase-form torso of Figure 80, became so familiar to Rodin that he could easily have produced many versions without recourse to a model or tracing.

Thus Type II is not simply a group of variant Type I life drawings, but a distinctly separate, parallel mode. Type II is the simultaneous adjunct of Type I, the product of direct distillation rather than stylistic evolution. Type I and Type II represent the two stages of the initial conception of the later manner, as explained previously; examples of both types can be dated before 1900.[132]

The third category is a looser classification, which includes the remainder of Rodin's later drawings. Type III, exemplified by aquarelles, such as Figure 81, and pencil drawings, such as Figure 82, represents a retreat from the dual extremes of Types I and II. Distortions are reduced, but the figure is not conceived in one-line simplicity. The pencil line moves rapidly but has neither the multiple irregularities of a Type I line nor the wiry fineness of a Type II. The line is less tense; *pentimenti*, when they occur, are grouped more closely along normative lines and are less frenetic. While Type I does not presuppose the wash effect at all, and Type II depends on the solidity afforded by it, a Type III watercolor mingles developed pencil working and wash with a greater attention to atmospheric effects and modeled volumes (*Fig. 81*). One group within this third classification is distinguished by its markedly larger scale and distinct paper type, appearing on sheets of cream-colored, laid paper, generally 15 inches tall by 9¼ inches wide; a rougher surface on this paper gives the stroking a grainy visual texture.

Type III drawings have the appearance, then, of more standard forms of life-drawing apparently done by looking at both the sheet and the model. This different handling, and the fact that poses are generally less active in Type III (concordances in poses between this latter group and the previous two have yet to be found) distinguish it as distinctly separate from the original research (Type I) and synthesis (Type II) conceptions of the later manner. No drawing in this third manner can be dated to 1900 or before. Rodin apparently came to this approach after 1900, and, though it may be initially more attractive in an ordinary sense, it is finally less interesting.

The development of the Type III mode parallels Rodin's growing attraction to muted effects, visible in such later marbles as the head of Puvis de Chavannes. In 1913, Gustave Coquiot, denying that Rodin did all of his drawings without looking at the paper, described "hundreds and hundreds of pencil drawings," carefully worked up, "done conscientiously, with extreme loving care." Rodin had apparently hung many of these in a separate room of the Hôtel Biron (the present Musée Rodin;

Rodin held space there from 1907 on).[133] These must have been the same drawings Paul Gsell described in 1910; "More recently, Rodin, continuing to use pencil, has stopped modeling with the brush. He has become satisfied with indicating shading by stomping the contour lines with his finger. The silvery gray rubbing envelops the forms like a cloud; it renders them lighter and seemingly unreal."[134]

Certainly the taste for such effects (*Figs. 82 and 83*) was not a sudden development. Aquarelles dating before 1907 display heavy stomping,[135] and the sensibility is clearly evident in a 1905 drawing from sculpture (*Fig. 84*). Rodin had been in the habit of stomping contour lines, if only to subdue erratic *pentimenti*, since 1900.[136] Though there is no stomping in the two pencil drawings in the National Gallery in Washington, which can be dated July, 1908 (*Figs. 85 and 86*), there is a stroked shading system not unlike that of Figure 82, stabilizing the internal volumes of the body and suggesting a refleshing of the original Type I mode.

After 1900, the chronology of Rodin's drawings profits from records available in exhibition catalogues, illustrated publications, and numerous descriptions. However, the doubts surrounding the exact dating of the softened pencil drawings are only one example of the way in which these records fail to answer all questions. Consecutive *terminus* dates can be established for a sizable number of drawings, yet the resultant order may be meaningless. Figure 78, for instance, appeared on the cover of a book in 1908;[137] yet a drawing showing the same pose was published in 1900 (*Figs. 62 and 126*). In this case, as in many others, the same pose is known in both Type I (*Fig. 126*) and Type II (*Fig. 62*) manifestations; furthermore, some Type II drawings have been seen in two or three virtually identical manifestations, and the interval between original conception and later variation is impossible to assess.

When one finally puts all the datable drawings of the late manner together, it seems that, with the exception of the very heavily stomped pencil drawings and possibly the Type III aquarelles, all of the most significant changes in Rodin's draftsmanship had been made by 1900, and the question of dates for many individual pieces thereafter is thus largely academic. This is not to say that he only reworked previous drawings and motifs, though this practice undoubtedly did continue. However, in approach, all of Rodin's later graphic work is dependent on conclusions reached in the 1890's, and later modifications of style are, if anything, slightly retrograde.

Yet it cannot consequently be inferred that drawing was less important to the artist as he grew older; on the contrary, he became more and more attracted to it. After the uproar provoked by *Balzac* in the 1890's and especially after his one-man retrospective at the Universal Exposition of 1900, Rodin became not only a man of considerable wealth

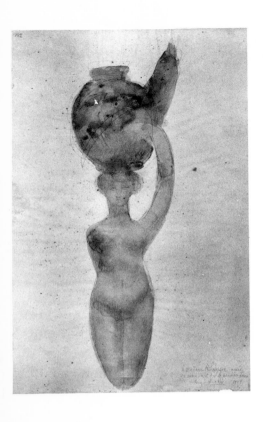

80. *Kneeling Nude with Vase on Her Head*, c. 1900–1905.
Lead pencil, watercolor wash. 19¾ x 12½ inches. National
Gallery of Art, Washington, D.C. Gift of Mrs. John W.
Simpson.

81. *Seated Nude*, c. 1902–10. Lead pencil, watercolor
wash. 9⅞ x 8⅝ inches. The Stanford Museum of Art,
Stanford, California. B. G. Cantor Foundation.

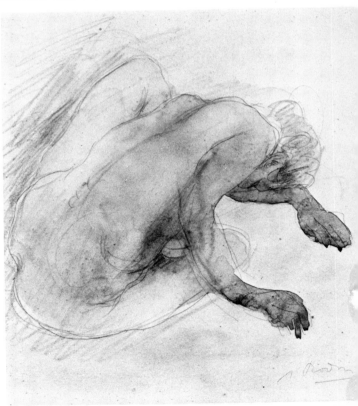

82. *Standing Nude*, c. 1908–14. Lead pencil.
12⁹⁄₃₂ x 7¹⁵⁄₁₆ inches. Collection of the John
and Mable Ringling Museum of Art, Sara-
sota, Florida.

83. *Study of a Female Nude Figure (Satyr-
ess)*, 1905–8. Lead pencil. 9¾ x 12⅝ inches.
The Metropolitan Museum of Art, New
York. Gift of Georgia O'Keeffe, 1965.

Erratum

Figure 83 is printed upside down.

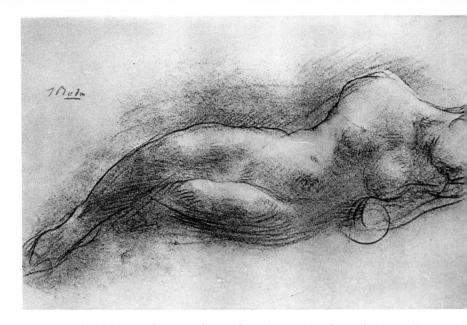

84. *Figure of a Woman* (drawing after sculpture), 1905. Lead pencil. Size and present l[oca]tion unknown. Reproduced from *Gazette des Beaux-Arts*, June, 1905.

85. *Seated Nude*, 1908. Lead pencil. 12¼ x 7⅞ inches (sheet folded—full width 15¾ inches). National Gallery of Art, Washington, D.C. Gift of Mrs. John W. Simpson.

86. *Seated Nude*, 1908. Lead pencil. 12¼ x 7⅞ inches (sheet folded—full width 15¾ inches). National Gallery of Art, Washington, D.C. Gift of Mrs. John W. Simpson.

87. *Cambodian Dancers*, 1906. Lead pencil, watercolor wash. 10¾/16 x 7¹³/16 inches. Museum Boymans-van Beuningen, Rotterdam.

but also an international artistic celebrity. With the diversions of his new status and with increasing age (Rodin was sixty in 1900) there was a marked decline in the sculptor's ability to realize the kind of monumental groups that occupied him in previous decades. Instead, he became increasingly the editor of his own works, watching over a team of assistants who produced to order new casts and carvings of the conceptions of earlier years. Rodin's personal creative energies found their outlet largely in portrait busts, in such smaller studies as his series of sculptures of dancers,[138] and in drawing. Sufficiently affluent to be free from concern over the fees of his models, he passed more and more time in drawing. The great majority of the roughly 7,200 sheets now in the Musée Rodin collection are in the later manner; with the many aquarelles found in collections around the world, they attest to a prodigious activity.

Among these later exercises, the drawings of Cambodian dancers, executed in the summer of 1906, are of particular note.[139] Unlike other rapid life-drawings of the late manner which, like Figure 61, "read" the complexities of body form, the Cambodian series (Figures 87, 88, and Color Plate II are examples) evinces little concern for bone structure. Rodin smoothed arms and shoulders into more tubular shapes (*Figs. 87 and 132*), the better to emphasize the continuity of a serpentine undulation of the dancers' upper quarters that he found particularly fascinating.[140] Of the artist's little dancer sculptures of 1910–12[141] (whose models are thought to have been can-can girls), Leo Steinberg remarked, "Rodin's modeling blinds itself to external anatomy, projecting instead the rhythm of his own working hands, . . . and the lines of an intuited movement."[142] In the broad sweeps of pencil and brush that render the Cambodians as ciphers of movement (*Fig. 87*), these drawings, and some contemporary figure studies as well (*Fig. 77*),[143] anticipate the sculptures by several years.

Some of the same tendencies can be seen in the pieces that were, by contrast to the much-remarked Cambodian series, the least known of Rodin's later drawings: the *découpages*, or cut-outs (*Fig. 89*). These were never remarked, and apparently never exhibited or published, until quite recently. Robert Descharnes published several, and dated them about 1908–15.[144] However, several similar pieces are part of a Princeton University collection formed by René Chéruy, one of Rodin's secretaries, between 1902 and 1908.[145] The *découpages* were apparently play elements for the artist, allowing him to arrange new assemblages of selected figures. He did this either by gluing down the fragments themselves on a separate sheet (Figure 89 is such an assemblage) or, possibly, by using them as stencil patterns to transfer the shapes in pencil. This latter idea was suggested by Madame Chéruy,[146] and the appearance of the silhouette of the lower body in Figure 89 in a 1902 reproduction, combined with a spatially unrelated figure (*Fig. 90*) supports the hypothesis. The *découpage* was not solely a late phenomenon in Rodin's graphic work;

Figure 91, from the Goupil ensemble, shows that, as early as the 1880's, Rodin sometimes resolved the complexities of a drawing by cutting out the essential shape he was after—a shape whose silhouette may fail to correspond to that of the drawing itself.

It would be wrong to distinguish the *découpages* as the private side of Rodin's later graphic work; despite the publicity they received, all the later drawings, like the great majority of their predecessors, were first and foremost private sources of education and pleasure for the artist. Though this opens up the broader question of Rodin's attitude toward his work, there is a chronological problem involved as well. Anthony Ludovici, Rodin's secretary in 1906–7, once asserted, and other writers have agreed, that Rodin originally thought his drawings to be of little importance, and only changed his evaluation very late in life, when he naïvely came to be convinced by the praise of his admirers.[147] This line of thinking may be taken to explain the large separate exhibitions of his drawings Rodin authorized—in 1907 and 1908 in Paris, in 1908 and 1910 at Stieglitz's "291" Gallery in New York, in 1911 in Lyons, and so on. However, it fails to explain why, in 1906, Rodin was so concerned with public misunderstanding of his drawings that he asked Bourdelle to write an article on them,[148] or why, in the retrospectives of 1898 and 1900, he displayed them prominently. A distinction that may help to resolve these questions is that between understanding and aesthetic admiration.

Rodin believed that a drawing was "beautiful" only in terms of the feelings that it conveyed, and felt that the only good "style" was one that effaced itself to this end.[149] He was perhaps baffled, then, when flocks of admirers came to praise the beauty of his later drawings. He exhibited his drawings not to provoke such admiration, but to instruct, as he explained to Bourdelle. "As my drawings are more free," he wrote, "they will give more liberty to artists who study them, not in telling them to do likewise, but in showing them their own genius and giving wings to their own impulse, in showing them the enormous space in which they can develop."[150] His belief in the importance of the late drawings in this latter, more significant sense, was hardly the later development Ludovici claims but dates to the conception of the mode itself. In discussing the late drawings in 1898, Charles Quentin reported that Rodin considered them "the synthesis of his life's work, the outcome of all his labor and knowledge."[151]

Guided by the academic belief that the nude figure was the truest medium for the expression of human thought and emotion, Rodin's development as a draftsman was a search for expressive gesture. When, in his early years, his mind was filled with literary motifs of passion and suffering, or with optimistic visions of idyllic fertility, he sought suitable poses and styles in his imagination, and in the art of the past. In

88. *Cambodian Dancer*, 1906. Lead pencil, gouache. 11¾ x 7½ inches. Rodin Museum, Philadelphia Museum of Art. Given by Jules Mastbaum.

89. *Two Cut-out Figures*, c. 1900–1906. Lead pencil, watercolor wash. Lower figure 13½ inches high; upper figure 13 inches high; glued on sheet with third figure; full sheet 22½ x 28½ inches. Princeton University Library, Princeton, New Jersey.

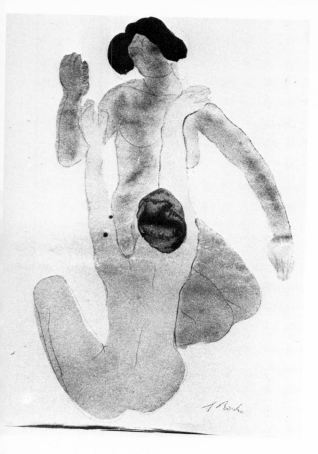

90. Illustration for Octave Mirbeau's *Le Jardin des Supplices* (Paris, 1902), c. 1898–99. Color lithograph. 12⅞ x 9¹⁵⁄₁₆ inches.

91. *Centaur Carrying a Woman (Le Sabbat)*, c. 1885. Pen and ink, watercolor, gouache (cut out and mounted). 7½ x 9 inches (size of full sheet). Rodin Museum, Philadelphia Museum of Art. Given by Jules Mastbaum.

1875, Michelangelo's force revealed to him the limitations of the formulas he had followed, and he tried briefly to assimilate this experience by copying Michelangelesque poses directly. Then, in the gouache drawings, as in the early *Gates* sculptures, he reconstituted the figures derived from his research of the 1860's and 1870's, revitalizing them in more dramatic facture. He came to see, however, that the expressive quality he had so admired in Michelangelo was dependent on movements and emotions that could not be found in traditional sources, but only in nature. Rodin then had to unlearn not only a lifetime of acquired gestural conventions, but also a basic approach to art. For, believing finally that the spirit of the human form was most clearly revealed in its most instinctive and ephemeral gestures, he saw that his drawings could no longer be based on a conscious domination of means, and that only a style reduced to its most essential elements could transmit such perceptions. Thus Rodin achieved his most personal draftsmanship through willful self-effacement, and the late drawings reflect at the same time the summation of his knowledge, a conscious forgetting, and an unceasing desire to learn.

NOTES

1. Judith Cladel, *Rodin, sa vie glorieuse et inconnue* (Paris: Grasset, Edition Définitive, 1950), p. 26.

2. H. E. C. Dujardin-Beaumetz, "Rodin's Reflections on Art," in Albert Elsen (ed.), *Auguste Rodin: Readings on his Life and Work* (Englewood Cliffs, N.J.: Prentice-Hall, 1965), p. 161.

3. The drawing collection at the Musée Rodin in Paris contains roughly 7,200 numbers. The numbers are written on the drawings and are accompanied by an oval *cachet* enclosing the letters M. R, and measuring one half inch in maximum length. Each number does not always represent a separate sheet; one sheet may contain five or ten catalogue numbers on its recto and verso. On the other hand, many verso drawings are not numbered, and several small figure studies on a sheet are often grouped under one number. Hereafter, when drawings are referred to by catalogue numbers, such numbers are not to be confused with numerical references that relate to Georges Grappe's catalogue of the Musée Rodin collection, which is almost solely a catalogue of the sculpture. The numerical sequence in the drawings catalogue is not chronological. Though an effort was made to include only early works in the first 350 entries, sheets dating to 1875 are found in that range, and some student works occur as late as the 5100 range of the numbering.

The number of drawings in other collections is unknown, and certainly the attributions include numerous forgeries; however, judging by the frequency with which Rodin drawings appear on the art market, there is a very sizable body of Rodin drawings in private hands around the world.

4. A prime example of this is the gouache drawing in the Louvre (RF 30146), dedicated in 1897 but clearly done in the previous decade (see *Dessins de Sculpteurs de Pajou à Rodin*, catalogue of an exhibition at the Cabinet des Dessins of the Louvre, Paris, 1964, pl. 23). A notable exception is the pencil drawing in the National Gallery in Washington, D.C. (B-486), inscribed "drawing done this morning July 7, 1908."

5. "He related that, very young, as far back as his memory went, he drew; his first models were the paper sacks, made with the pages of illustrated books in which the grocer whom his mother patronized wrapped his prunes. The Rodin Museum possesses some of these stammering efforts of childhood that Rodin had carefully preserved." (Léonce Bénédite, *Rodin* [Paris: F. Rieder, 1926], p. 7.)

6. Robert Descharnes published, on page 24 of his *Rodin* (New York: Viking, 1967), Musée Rodin drawing no. 132, which he identified as a sketch from life, done at the Paris horse market. It is, rather, a copy after a detail of a lithograph by Géricault, *Rouliers montant une côte* (LD 76); Musée Rodin no. 120 is done from the same scene; both drawings are on a cheap browned wove paper of a type not seen elsewhere in the student works, and their heavy-handed ineptitude sets them apart from the copy work attributable to the period of instruction at the Petite Ecole.

7. "Auguste Rodin was placed in a school directed by the Brothers [of the Christian Doctrine] which occupied a building . . . in the rue Val-de-Grâce; he stayed there up to age nine." (Judith Cladel, *Rodin, sa vie*, p. 71.) Cladel and others related that Rodin learned virtually nothing here; however, it should be noted that the Brothers of the Christian Doctrine were involved in art education and, in fact, ran a drawing school at the same location, in the rue Val-de-Grâce. See the evaluation of drawing schools in *Le Beau dans l'Utile* (Paris: Union Centrale des Arts Decoratifs, 1866) and the comments of Horace Lecoq de Boisbaudran in *Coup-d'Oeil sur l'enseignement des Beaux-arts* (Paris: Morel, 1879), p. 17.

8. In the morning, Rodin drew at the Petite Ecole. In the afternoon, he drew from the antiques in the Louvre and then went to the print room of the Imperial Library to copy from albums of gravures. From 5 to 8 at night, he drew from the live model at the Gobelins studio. At night, he reworked the sketches he had done during the day, drawing even at the dinner table. (Judith Cladel, *Rodin, sa vie*, p. 78.)

9. Dujardin-Beaumetz, in Elsen (ed), *Readings*, p. 177.

10. In the context of this chronology, we cannot stop to give a separate, integral treatment of Lecoq and all the implications of his method of instruction. For this, the reader is directed to Albert Elsen's discussion of Lecoq and his influence on Rodin in *Rodin* (New York: Museum of Modern Art, 1963), pp. 160–62.

11. Albert Boime, *The Academy and French Painting in the Nineteenth Century* (New York: Phaidon, 1970), pp. 24–36. Boime outlines the basic technique of suggesting relief through parallel lines closely juxtaposed (*see Fig. 2*), and the adjunct use of either cross-hatching or the *estompe* (stomp). All three of these methods appear in the early drawings in the Musée Rodin, and the trend of progress seems to be from the parallels, through the *hachure*, to the stomp in more proficient works.

12. Boime, *The Academy*, remarks on this, and it is also confirmed by Lecoq's comment: "I am not unaware . . . that there exists today great opposition to drawn or engraved models, particularly against those of the figure or figure fragments." (Horace Lecoq Boisbaudran, *Lettres à un jeune professeur* [Paris: Morel, 1876], p. VIII.)

13. There are eight small pen and sepia studies of Parthenon sculpture in the Musée Rodin (maximum height 5⁹⁄₁₆ inches, maximum width 6¾ inches); they are on tracing paper, with occasional indications of preliminary pencil work. To this number should be added two pencil and watercolor wash drawings (both unfinished) of sections of the frieze.

14. See the decorative scene, in tondo format, Musée Rodin no. 1, published by Descharnes, *Rodin*, p. 16. Musée Rodin no. 109, in the same technique and format, depicts a similar scene, and a copy after an illustration of antique architecture, no. 105, has the same fine lines and pale tonalities of wash. Musée Rodin no. 106, after a painting or an illustration, depicts a two-personage mythological banishment scene in a similar vein.

15. The copy after Le Sueur, no. 240, is in pencil; it does not include the background of the painting. The Poussin scene, no. 296, is in charcoal, heightened with white chalk. Both paintings are in the Louvre.

16. There are two life studies in the sketchbook (see Note 20, below) from the Mastbaum Collection, which is now owned by Mrs. Jefferson Dickson. In the Musée Rodin in Paris, there is one small life-study nearly identical with those in the sketchbook (see Note 23, below). In addition, Grappe lists thirteen large *académies* in his 1931 catalogue of the Musée Rodin, p. 27; my own research there, however, indicates that Grappe included in this count the oil-on-canvas *académies* (see Descharnes, *Rodin*, p. 17, for an illustration of such a painted study). Only five true drawings of models (six, including the small *pochade* mentioned in Note 23, below) were found in the collection. The five large *académies* include the two males seen in Figures 4 and 5, two other males, and one female; the latter, surprisingly neoclassical in feeling, was exhibited in the 1967 exhibition *Rodin* at the Villa Medici, Rome, cat. no. 3a.

17. T. H. Bartlett, "Auguste Rodin, Sculptor," in Elsen (ed.), *Readings*, p. 19.

18. There are four studies of human anatomy in the Musée Rodin: the two illustrated here (*Fig. 6*), one other skeleton, and an *écorché* head. There is a similar *écorché* horse's head, one sheet showing four studies of a horse's leg, skeletal and *écorché*, and a horse skeleton, published by Descharnes, *Rodin*, p. 25. The latter is the most proficient of all of them in its handling of structure and atmospheric effects.

19. Among the things Rodin specifically mentioned drawing from at the Museum of Natural History were anatomical fragments, and two Musée Rodin drawings, no. 98 and no. 142, show lion paws. Miss Cladel relates that Rodin also attended anatomical courses at the Medical School (*Rodin, sa vie*, p. 86). In regard to the studies of wild animals, Camille Mauclair related that Rodin went to their cages at 6 A.M. to draw them, during the period of his study under Barye. (*Auguste Rodin, l'homme et l'oeuvre* [Paris: Renaissance du Livre, 1918], p. 1.)

20. This sketchbook is now the property of Mrs. Jefferson Dickson, and is on loan to the Philadelphia Museum of Art. There are thirty-seven pages

with drawings (thirty-five numbered), all about 3¾ x 5⅞ inches on wove paper, seven-thousandths of an inch thick. All pages save four are white; pages 31 and 34 are toned light gray, and 32 and 33 are toned light brown. The work is done for the most part in pen and sepia, or pencil. As this book goes to press, Professor Jacques de Caso of the University of California at Berkeley is preparing to publish, in *Master Drawings*, a complete descriptive article on the Mastbaum sketchbook.

21. A letter from Judith Cladel to the art dealers F. and J. Tempelaere, dated July 5, 1926, now in the Philadelphia Free Library.

22. Miss Cladel's description is riddled with discrepancies. Rodin worked in Barye's course in 1863–64, when he was twenty-three and twenty-four years old. This would not have been the same period in which he was constantly drawing at the print room. In other, similar descriptions, Miss Cladel refers to the book copied from as *L'Histoire de Costume Romain* rather than *Le Costume dans L'Antiquité*, and places it at the Imperial Library rather than at the Louvre. A search of the collections of the old Imperial Library has so far failed to yield sources for Rodin's copies. Nevertheless, Miss Cladel is correct, I believe, when she connects the little album with the period of the Barye instruction. Not only the drawings of wild animals, but also the studies of horses (at the Boulevard St.-Marcel market) have always been associated with these years. Also, a quick sketch of animal paws on page 3 recto of the album corresponds to drawings of anatomical fragments discussed in Note 19 above.

Jacques de Caso, who generously permitted me to read a manuscript of his long study of the student sketchbook (see Note 20 above), believes that some of the work in the album should be assigned to the period prior to Rodin's work at the Petite Ecole; his argument that nothing in the book reflects any known aspect of the school curriculum is convincing but coincides equally well with the proposition that the work was done after, rather than before, the school years. Apparently, he does not find the connections with descriptions of Rodin's 1864 work as compelling as I do. He further feels that many of the drawings are to be assigned to a second period of work, at a later, unspecified date in Rodin's maturity. Given Rodin's drawing habits, it seems more logical that he would have filled the album completely in a short period. I find it unlikely that Rodin would have carried with him an old student sketchbook for the purpose of making studies in his mature years.

The sketchbook was out of the artist's hands for an unspecified stretch of time, as he gave it to Auguste Cheffer, his cousin. The signature on the last page, dated 1916, apparently corresponds to the efforts to gather and organize all of Rodin's work for the Paris Musée Rodin, and to the artist's efforts to regain the sketchbook, as described by Judith Cladel in *Rodin, sa vie*, p. 73; it is not unlikely that the cousin (who was unwilling to release the album for the museum, despite the artist's request and offer of a statue in trade), thinking of Rodin's impending death, brought the album to him to have the provenance more securely asserted in this fashion.

23. There are several sheets in the Musée Rodin that do correspond to more informal work in the sketchbook. One, no. 58, is nearly identical in size and handling to the life study on page 12 of the sketchbook, and looks to have been done from the same model, with the pose reversed. Four other sketches

show the kind of figure style and pen-work seen in many of the Mastbaum sheets, and three deal with figures in military costumes of the late eighteenth century. Judith Cladel (*Rodin, sa vie*, p. 73) related that the Musée Rodin possessed similar whole sketchbooks, but Madame Cécile Goldscheider, the present *Conservateur*, has assured me that no such sketchbooks exist in the collection now.

24. In 1912, Rodin exclaimed to an audience: "How can I express to you the emotion that we felt, young students at the drawing school in the rue de L'Ecole de Medecine, when Carpeaux, as instructor, passed to correct the strongest of us? . . . Oh! the adoration we felt for him!" ("Carpeaux jugé par Rodin," in *Le Temps*, June 15, 1912.)

25. *Ibid.* "Do you see the grace which springs forth and fills everything with its charms? It is the old architecture of the eighteenth century." Later, Rodin said of Carpeaux: "His sculpture had the lively and dashing aspect of his fellow countryman Watteau." (Dujardin-Beaumetz in Elsen [ed.], *Reading*, p. 181.)

26. There are fourteen works in this vein in the Musée Rodin, including a sketch of a desert landscape in light watercolors. Ten of them are of the same type as Figure 13: small copies in either pencil or sepia on tracing paper, sometimes worked over with wash.

27. This self-portrait was published by Descharnes, *Rodin*, p. 10. There is evidence of a certain shyness and effeminacy, perhaps the result of his mother's highly developed piety, in some of Cladel's descriptions of Rodin's youth (Cladel, *Rodin, sa vie*, pp. 74, 82).

28. Cladel related (*Ibid.*, p. 81), "By the soft domination of Boucher and Van Loo, of Clodion and Houdon, whose works he copied so often, Rodin was the student of the eighteenth century honored at the Petite Ecole, while scorned at the Grande. The supple facture of the candidate was contrary to the dryness of surface modeling extolled by all the professors [of the Ecole des Beaux-Arts], disciples of David." (*Ibid.*, p. 81).

29. Evidence of Rodin's attraction to eroticism in the eighteenth-century vein is provided by a Musée Rodin drawing, no. 75, that shows two female nudes dancing with a satyr, observed by a small *amor*. The nudes are very much in the mannered proportions and style of some of the Mastbaum sketchbook figures; one has her left hand in the satyr's groin, as he in turn reaches back to clasp the buttocks of the other dancer with his left hand.

30. "Jules Klagmann, whose name is too completely forgotten, was nonetheless an original physiognomy of his time, though he only occupied a second-rank position in the Ecole. He belonged, like Maindron, to the little group of sculptors formed outside of academic doctrines and deeply penetrated by the ideas of romanticism. He modeled little figures in bronze by which he manifested his worship of the great literary divinities of romanticism: Dante, Shakespeare, and Lord Byron." (Léonce Bénédite, *Rodin*, p. 11.)

31. One of Lecoq's students remarked, "obeying a scruple which will no doubt seem exaggerated, he never let any of his work be seen by his pupils, not wishing to thus expose them to the temptation to imitate his manner." (Felix Régamey, *Horace Lecoq de Boisbaudran et ses élèves* [Paris: Champion, 1903], p. 6.)

32. A reading of Régamey's account makes it clear Bénédite was correct

in stating (*Rodin*, p. 8) that "Rodin did not regularly receive his [Lecoq's] counsel, and was not a part of his private studio group." As recounted to T. H. Bartlett, Rodin won a bronze medal for drawing from the cast at the age of fifteen, and a bronze medal for modeling and a silver medal for drawing from the antique at eighteen (Bartlett, in Elsen [ed.], *Readings*, p. 17).

33. Horace Lecoq de Boisbaudran, *Coup-d'Oeil sur l'enseignement des Beaux-Arts*, p. 34.

34. Bartlett, in Elsen (ed.), *Readings*, pp. 19–20.

35. Dujardin-Beaumetz in Elsen (ed.), *Readings*, p. 154.

36. "He regards the time spent with his new employer [Carrier-Belleuse] as having been of great injury to him as an artist, and that, had it not been for the intense urgency of his temperament and his persistent habit of working at home from life, it would have ruined him." (Bartlett, in Elsen [ed], *Readings*, p. 26.)

37. Georges Grappe, then curator of the Musée Rodin, advanced this idea in "Classical Affinities of a Modern Master—Rodin's Drawings," in *Formes*, XXI (1932), 318–21. Grappe, of course, had free access to all the drawings in the Musée Rodin collection; he extended this privilege to his friend and fellow scholar Haavard Rostrup, who concurred with Grappe's ideas on the Dantesque drawings in his valuable study, "Les Dessins de Rodin," *From the Collection of the Ny Carlsberg Glyptotek* (1938), pp. 221–26.

38. Grappe, "Classical Affinities," p. 319, said that the Dantesque studies "follow directly the large charcoal sketches of his student days" in the museum collection.

39. Bartlett, in Elsen (ed.), *Readings*, p. 26.

40. This is a personal observation based on the study in the Musée Rodin. One such fragment was published unreworked in the Goupil publication, *Les Dessins d'Auguste Rodin* (Paris: Boussod, Manzi, Joyant & Cie., 1897), pl. 47. Judging from the specifically Michelangelesque pose and broader generalization of volume, it would appear to date about 1876–80.

41. The strain of Christian iconography present in this phase of Rodin's work is a subject I hope to deal with in a future study. Particularly frequent are groups having a connection with the Last Supper.

42. "Among the large studies made by the sculptor in Brussels, in the development of his principles of composition, was a group called 'Ugolino,' but he was not satisfied with it, and destroyed all save the body of the principal figure." (Bartlett, in Elsen [ed.], *Readings*, p. 23.)

43. Judith Cladel relates that Rodin realized his own ignorance at the Petite Ecole. To remedy this, he read Hugo, Musset, Lamartine, Homer, Virgil, and Dante. The latter apparently "branded his young imagination." (*Rodin, sa vie*, p. 79.)

44. T. H. Bartlett recounted that, while at boarding school in Beauvais, Rodin passed "most of his time in drawing fanciful designs, telling stories, and reciting imaginary descriptions to his comrades." (Bartlett, in Elsen [ed.], *Readings*, p. 16.)

45. A predecessor of this composition, Musée Rodin no. 404, is a direct copy of the composition of an entombment relief from the Church of St. Eustache in Paris. This relief, currently assigned to the French School of the sixteenth century and much in the style of Goujon, is now in the Louvre collection.

46. Elsen (*Rodin*, p. 162) convincingly connects the "flayed" appearance of many of the imaginative drawings with one of Lecoq's methods of instruction, in which the student drew the figure by first accentuating bone projections and then the outlines of all the muscles; the style may also relate to the *écorché* figure models that were a common accessory of artists' studios at the time. The origin of the over-muscled body type is a matter of speculation. Certain figures in John Flaxman's illustrations for Dante, which Rodin certainly knew, show similar proportions. Carpeaux's etched study for *Ugolino* shows another derivation of what is at base most probably a late Michelangelo figure type. In characterizing these drawings, it should be remembered that Rodin preserved only certain fragments and discarded many others; so we see the earlier work, even when not retouched, through the filter of his later sensibility.

47. It is paradoxical that, mingled with this enormously bulky type of figure drawing, and apparently dating to the same time, is a series of tiny, spritelike figures, whose poses are those of acrobats bending, lunging, and jumping. All the emphasis in these curious figures is on *élan* of movement, and the body is treated often in a single curve. See *Rodin*, catalogue of an exhibition, Villa Medici, Rome, 1967, fig. 60.

48. Grappe, "Classical Affinities," p. 320.

49. In the preface to a later book, *Auguste Rodin l'homme et l'oeuvre* (Paris: La Renaissance du Livre, 1918), Mauclair describes the way in which his 1898 article, "L'Art de M. Auguste Rodin," *Revue des Revues* (June 15, 1898), pp. 597–610, was approved by the artist. Mauclair was invited to speak on Rodin at the artist's one-man show at the Universal Exposition of 1900.

50. The article, entitled "Notes sur la technique et le symbolisme de M. Auguste Rodin," is known to me through a clipping copy preserved in the Louis Vauxcelles collection of press and periodical clippings at the Doucet Library of Art and Archaeology in Paris. No date appears with the article, though it would seem to have been written after 1900 and before the artist's death. The periodical name on the page opposite the article's title is *La Renaissance Latine*. The French word *esquisse*, here translated as "sketch," could refer to either a sculptural or a drawn image; Mauclair does not specify.

51. Among the rare drawings that do seem to be direct projects for sculpture is a sheet of pencil studies, one group of which has been reworked, in pen and sepia, into what appears to be a sketch for *La Défense*. In this sketch, on the Musée Rodin sheet no. 226, the winged figure clutches a falling personage to her chest with her left hand, while the right hand is held, fist turned out, against her forehead. The style of this sheet is one of rapid, summary notations, having little in common with the Dantesque sheets; it is also on a different paper type. See also the discussion of source drawings for *The Gates* in Note 81.

52. Camille Mauclair, "Notes sur la technique et le symbolisme de M. Auguste Rodin," p. 208.

53. Elsen published two of the three Boulevard Anspach caryatids, and noted their relation to Puget, in *Rodin*, pp. 15, 16. Descharnes published all three, and cited as a source the caryatids of the Maison du Renard of the Grand Palais in Brussels, in his *Rodin*, pp. 42, 43. Rodin's familiarity with these figures no doubt dates back to 1864–65, when he worked with Jules Dalou on the decoration of the Hotel Païva in Paris. In the large dining-room

fireplace here, as well as in a console in the large salon, Dalou used caryatids derived from those of Puget. See Arsène Houssaye, *Un Hôtel Célèbre sous le Second Empire* (Paris: Cubat, 1896), pp. 5, 21.

For a broader consideration of Michelangelo's influence on Rodin, see Joseph Gantner, *Rodin und Michelangelo* (Vienna: Schroll, 1953), and also, most especially for Rodin's Belgian work, Albert Alhadeff's article "Michelangelo and the Early Rodin," *Art Bulletin*, XLV (1963), 363–67.

54. Bartlett, in Elsen (ed.), *Readings*, p. 30.

55. *Ibid.* (The figures on this monument are considered in depth by Alhadeff in "Michelangelo and the Early Rodin.")

56. *Ibid.*

57. An undated letter from Rodin to Rose Beuret, quoted by Cladel in *Rodin, sa vie*, pp. 111–12.

58. Alhadeff cites only the three drawings published by Gantner in *Rodin und Michelangelo*, and was perhaps unaware that there are four sheets in the group. Alhadeff cites his reasoning for attributing the drawings to Rodin's student years in a lengthy note in "Michelangelo and the Early Rodin," pp. 365–66. He says, "stylistically these drawings suggest an earlier date than 1875. The figures are modeled by means of light and shadow. The finished quality of these drawings is in marked contrast to the schematic style of the late 1870's." He concludes that "the most conclusive argument for dating them in the late 1850's, when Rodin was still an adolescent, is the absence of any reference to *la grande ligne*, the system uppermost in Rodin's mind in 1875."

Plaster casts of the tomb figures existed in Paris, so Rodin could have done these studies either before or after his Italian trip (see Note 61, below).

59. Clément Janin, in "Les Dessins de Rodin," *Les Maîtres Artistes*, (October 15, 1903), p. 285, notes the similarities between these drawings and student work, but specifically dates them in 1877. "Other drawings," he said, "after Michelangelo and the antique, though the artist was 37 [when he did them], are not significantly different from his first ones [student drawings]." Another biographer also asserted that they were done after the return to Paris, mentioning "five drawings after Michelangelo executed in the chapel of the *Ecole des Beaux-Arts*." This count may include the faun's head discussed in Note 60, or a lost study of the Medici tomb figure *Dusk*. (Léon Riotor, *Rodin* [Paris: Alcan, 1927], p. 17.) Gantner accepts the 1875 dating, as does Madame Cécile Goldscheider, in *Rodin*, catalogue of an exhibition, Villa Medici, Rome, 1967, cat. no. 4; this apparently indicates they believe the drawings were done in the sacristy itself. Georges Grappe showed hesitation on this point; in the 1929 catalogue of the Musée Rodin, he listed them as dating from 1877, but then changed his mind in the 1931 edition, and dated them 1875. In 1932, in the article "Classical Affinities," he expressed, in a note on p. 319, indecision as to whether the drawings were done *in situ* or from the casts in Paris.

60. I believe there is a possibility that the *Dawn* (Fig. 20) was done at a date different from that of other views, such as the *Day* published by Descharnes (*Rodin*, p. 48). The *Dawn* treats a more dramatic and difficult viewpoint, and appears to be rendered more freely, with darker accents and more confident lines; furthermore, it corresponds to the profile view of the studies done on the trip to Italy. Since Rodin's letter from Florence, quoted above,

indicates that he knew the plasters, but also that he was unfamiliar with the side viewpoint seen in the *Dawn* drawing, there are some grounds for the hypothesis that the five drawings may result from two different encounters, one before, one after the Italian trip.

A drawing of the sculpted head of a faun, Musée Rodin, no. 5111, was published in *Rodin*, catalogue of an exhibition, Villa Medici, Rome, 1967, pl. 11; though not dated in that catalogue, the head was associated with the *Vatican Faun*, and with the four Michelangelo sheets, by Grappe in his 1931 Musée Rodin catalogue. I believe that the drawing of the faun's head is more probably a student work than any of the Michelangelo sheets, as its handling is much more tight and timid.

Alhadeff's reasoning in dating the sheets in the 1850's is weak at one important point. The fact that these drawings are fully developed in terms of *chiaroscuro* modeling does not reduce the possibility that they could have been done contemporaneously with the "schematic" imaginary drawings of the late 1870's. As we shall see throughout this study, Rodin changed modes of draftsmanship drastically, according to subject and purpose; certainly the eighteenth-century drawings and Sèvres studies dating from 1878–80, to be discussed in turn, have little to do with the "schematic" style either. If one date must be assigned to the four Michelangelo drawings together, I believe that date should be 1877.

61. The plaster casts of the tomb figures were installed in the *Musée de Petits-Augustins*, in 1837, but by Rodin's time they had been moved to the chapel of the Ecole des Beaux-Arts. They are discussed in an article cited by Alhadeff, Charles de Tolnay's " 'Michel-Ange dans son atelier' par Delacroix," *Gazette des Beaux-Arts* (1962), p. 43.

62. Musée Rodin nos. 268, 269, and 270 are all pencil sketches of the tomb of Lorenzo de' Medici. Nos. 268 and 269, not illustrated here, are drawn from a point closer to the front of the tomb, a three-quarter view also from the right side. Rodin seems to have been particularly interested in the compositional relationship between the silhouette of the *Dawn* and that of the seated *Lorenzo* behind and above her, as he restressed these lines in both the latter sketches.

63. The pages of this *carnet* were 4 x 2¹⁵⁄₁₆ inches when intact, a cheap, smooth wove paper, cream-colored and now showing light pulp chiving; the book was sewn-bound in four places along the long edge. Having only encountered these remnants in the months immediately before the deadline for this book, I propose to treat the sketchbook and its sources more thoroughly in a later article. The dominant figure in the sketchbook is that of Donatello's *Gattemalata* equestrian in Padua, of which there are nine studies from different viewpoints. Though Padua has not traditionally been included in Rodin's Italian itinerary, these sketches provide basis for the comment recorded later by Bartlett that "the equestrian statue, at Padua, is, in Rodin's estimation, the best one since the Greeks." Rodin also preserved a very light sketch of Donatello's *St. George* (Musée Rodin no. 186), a statue he told Bartlett was "all there is of Italian art, its sum and flower—an angel." (Bartlett, in Elsen [ed.], *Readings*, pp. 92–93.)

64. Head of *Moses*, Musée Rodin no. 160, torso of *Moses*, no. 192; *Rachel*, no. 189; *Leda*, no. 181. A large sheet, no. 178, separate from the

montage assemblages in which the sketchbook pages are found, has on its verso a small pen notation that suggests a wall of the sacristy, face on, with two consoles and seated figure in a niche above.

65. Judith Cladel, *Auguste Rodin pris sur la vie* (Paris: La Plume, 1903), p. 76.

66. Comparative measurements prove that these are tracings from the original life-study sheets. On this tendency in Rodin's sculpture, see Leo Steinberg's comments on "Assemblage and Graft" in *Rodin—Sculptures and Drawings*, catalogue of a traveling exhibition organized by the Slatkin Galleries, New York, 1963.

67. Cladel, *Auguste Rodin pris sur la vie*, p. 76.

68. All of the sanguine landscapes still visible are very much in the style of the one published by Descharnes, *Rodin*, p. 40, and resemble oil landscapes from the Belgian period. Grappe dated the latter 1872–76 in the 1931 Musée Rodin catalogue, no. 21.

69. The drawing of an Ugolino group, Musée Rodin no. 157, reproduced by Descharnes, *Rodin*, p. 88, is drawn on a section of a former montage sheet, now cut apart. The sketch, and the pencil studies around it, probably related to a drawing formerly laid down nearby.

70. The montage sheets could not have been made before 1875, as very early works mix and overlap the tracings from the life-drawings of models in Michelangelesque poses, and the sheets from the Italian sketchbook. It seems unlikely that they were assembled later than about 1877–78, as they include no drawings that seem to postdate the Michelangelesque poses. There is no sign that Dantesque drawings were ever laid down on such mount sheets. Many of the Dantesque sheets were pasted in a small bill-book, as described by Grappe in "Classical Affinities of a Modern Master."

71. Rodin's work at Sèvres was thoroughly documented and studied in Roger Marx's *Auguste Rodin, Céramiste* (Paris: Société de propagation des Livres d'Art, 1907). The Sèvres Museum now owns two vases by Rodin; however, as of this date, the drawings left to the museum are either misplaced or lost.

72. In *Rodin Céramiste*, p. 13, Marx describes the vase-related drawings given to Sèvres as "a series of sketches and tracings."

73. A large selection of Carrier-Belleuse's drawings can be found in the collection of ten loose-leafed portfolios published in Paris in 1884 by Goupil and Cie., under the title *Application de la figure humaine à la décoration et a l'ornementation industrielles*. H. W. Janson cites this publication and discusses Rodin's relationship with Carrier-Belleuse in "Rodin and Carrier-Belleuse; The Vase des Titans," *Art Bulletin*, L (September, 1968), pp. 278–80.

74. *L'Art* (1877), p. 198.

75. Roger Marx, "Cartons d'Artistes—Auguste Rodin," *L'Image* (September, 1897), p. 297.

76. Another study of *The Age of Bronze* was published by Léon Maillard in *Auguste Rodin, Statuaire* (Paris: Floury, 1899).

77. A personal reminiscence of such candlelight sessions, which have been remarked elsewhere, was given to me by Madame Antoine Bourdelle in a conversation in the summer of 1969.

78. Notable exceptions to the generalization advanced here are Carpeaux's drawings after his sculpture. The pen drawing of the bust of *Africa*, now in the Metropolitan Museum, corresponds closely to Rodin's hatching method.

79. Alhadeff has pointed out that 1875 was the four-hundredth anniversary of Michelangelo's birth, and that there were numerous drawings exhibitions staged in Florence for the occasion ("Michelangelo and the Early Rodin," p. 365). A pose on one of the sheets of life-studies of Michelangelesque gestures suggests that Rodin knew the pen sketch of a standing nude male turned to the right, in the Louvre collection.

80. *L'Art* (1880), p. 124. A variant of this drawing, in the same basic style and from the same point of view is in the collection of the Musée du Louvre; it was published by Descharnes in *Rodin*, p. 56. Another drawing of the *St. John*, a profile view washed with gouache, appeared in the *Catalogue Illustré du Salon*, 2d ed. (1881), p. 538, and was also reproduced in the *Revue des Revues* (June 15, 1898), p. 603.

81. There are a number of seated male figures that could be considered prototypes for *The Thinker* and also a great many embracing seated couples that suggest *The Kiss*. However, the closest relationship I know at present is that of Musée Rodin no. 5609, which shows almost exactly the bas-relief couple at the base of the right side panel of *The Gates*. This study is inscribed, "to make in a bas-relief group with the figurine crouching—Mephistos." The couple seen in bas-relief at the top of the left side panel of *The Gates* has a close prototype in Musée Rodin no. 1921. As both the drawings are on tracing paper and are rendered in fine-line articulation free from heavy wash, it seems very likely that they represent distillations of previous drawings.

The fact that many other Rodin drawings in the gouached manner bear inscriptions similar to that of no. 5609 but do not correspond to groups or figures now seen in *The Gates* is an indication that Rodin changed his method of work.

82. The artist was quoted by Serge Basset in "La Porte de L'Enfer," an article on the front page of the newspaper *Le Matin*, March 19, 1900. Elsen cites this article in a note on p. 290 of "Rodin's 'La Ronde,' " *Burlington Magazine* (June, 1965), pp. 290–99.

83. There are a great many studies for the architectural form of *The Gates* in the Musée Rodin collection. The full extent and nature of these preliminary thoughts may not be known for some time. The major and more detailed studies were published by Albert Elsen in *Rodin's Gates of Hell* (Minneapolis: University of Minnesota Press, 1960), and it is on these latter that I base my present comments.

84. The *Etudes* plate was a trial effort done soon after *Les Amours conduisant le monde*, in 1881, according to Delteil in *Le Peintre-Graveur Illustré*, VI (Paris: Delteil, 1910).

85. Haavard Rostrup, in "Les Dessins de Rodin," commented on the resemblance between the Lyons *Centaur* and Delacroix's *Education of Achilles*. The stylistic links between Rodin's drawings and those of other artists, both in terms of influence absorbed and influence passed on, are for the most part beyond the scope of the present chronological essay. I do not mean to ignore or deny these other considerations, however, but only to reserve comment, in

the hopes of establishing the most satisfactory chronological base for future, more comprehensive work. It is clear, for example, that there is a close relationship between Rodin's gouached drawings and those of Géricault, perhaps by way of Carpeaux as intermediary; Carpeaux's use of gouache and pen in his project for *Ugolino*, now in The Art Institute of Chicago, anticipates that of Rodin.

86. The reproductions appeared in an article on "Le Salon National," *L'Art* (1883), p. 38. Another drawing now in the Fogg Art Museum also figured in this group (Fogg 1943.912), as well as an intriguing drawing entitled "The Sculptor's Vision." Bartlett later reported that the latter drawing "indicates Rodin's entire life, and illustrates his whole character," and reported that the artist "proposes to execute this design for his own tomb." (Bartlett, in Elsen [ed.], *Readings*, p. 86.

87. Octave Mirbeau affirmed that Rodin "did not intend them to be made public," in his preface to the Goupil publication, *Les Dessins d'Auguste Rodin* (Paris: Boussod, Manzi, Joyant & Cie., 1897).

88. See for example the slight pen notations accompanying the inscription "Victor Hugo" on Musée Rodin no. 5616, published by Elsen in *Rodin's Gates of Hell*, pl. 34. My statement here is also based on several sheets with similar notations in the Musée Rodin collection.

89. See Loys Delteil, *Le Peintre-Graveur Illustré*, VI. Delteil cites the drypoints as being eleven in number; however, he excludes two. One of these was executed after the publication of his study, in 1916. This print was done for the American Hospital in Paris, which was treating facial wounds from the war. At the upper left, Rodin shows a mangled face, and at the lower right, the same face healed by surgery; between the two is a written form with a blank for addressee and signature, expressing thanks for a donation. Delteil also failed to remark a drypoint of which only one impression has ever been known; this is a *Dying Centaur*, interesting in its anticipation of Bourdelle's later statue of the same theme. It is illustrated in the sales catalogue of an auction held by Gilhofer and Ranschberg Ltd., Lucerne, on June 8–9, 1926, no. 329, p. 36. For a consideration of Rodin's drypoints in a different context, see Claude Roger-Marx, "Engravings by Sculptors in France," *Print Collector's Quarterly*, XVI, No. 2 (April, 1929), 145–64; Roger-Marx here calls Rodin's drypoints "the most important body of work engraved by a sculptor that exists."

90. Elsen suggests a source for the *Amours* in Fragonard's *Ronde des Amours*, or a variant thereof; see his "Rodin's 'La Ronde,' " p. 294.

91. Elsen has explored at length the iconography and meaning of *La Ronde* in his article "Rodin's 'La Ronde.' " Space does not permit a similar consideration here. The proscenium of *La Ronde* is closely related to the small drawing published in the Goupil volume, no. 122, pl. II; the group of dancing figures has prototypes too numerous to list among drawings in the Musée Rodin collection. The definitive drawing on which the print is based is now in a private collection in Paris; its owner kindly allowed me to study it. With the print's composition exact but, naturally, reversed, the drawing's background suggests that the scene is set either in a large, cathedral-like interior, or in a court with colonnades.

92. See plates in Marx, *Auguste Rodin, Céramiste*.

93. In his article "Les Pointes-sèches de M. Rodin," *Gazette des Beaux-Arts* (1902), p. 206, Roger Marx points out that Rodin's first five drypoints were unknown to the public until 1901, when Rodin was persuaded by a friend to exhibit *Bellone, Le Printemps,* and *La Ronde,* at the Salon of the National Society of Fine Arts.

94. The impression of this print owned by the National Gallery in Washington bears the artist's inscription, in the context of a dedication, "Portrait of Mme. Rodin."

95. These reproductions are found in Léon Maillard's *Auguste Rodin, Statuaire.* A double-view sketch of Hugo's head is reproduced at the end of Roger Marx's "Les Pointes-sèches de M. Rodin."

96. The method of first dotting out the path of a line dates back to Lecoq's training. When one set out to draw a line from one point to another, said Lecoq, it should not be done with a quick single stroke. "It is more certain," he said, "to prepare it first by a sequence of points more or less spaced out." (*Lettres à un jeune professeur,* p. 6.)

For Rodin's description of his encounter with Hugo, and for his use of Lecoq's memory-training in this case, see Dujardin-Beaumetz in Elsen (ed.), *Readings,* pp. 169–70. Rodin also described doing about sixty sketches of Hugo to Edmond de Goncourt, and he spoke of the effort he had made to avoid a conventionally idealized or invented image of Hugo, which the family would apparently have preferred; the conversation is in the Goncourt *Journal,* December 2, 1887.

97. These illustrations were drawn directly on the pages of a volume of the poetry. (As the three gouached drawings among them are not on text pages, they may have been done separately and inserted; however, I am convinced that they were executed at the same time as the others in any case.) There are 25 drawings, including a frontispiece and a bookplate couple at the end—two figures holding an escutcheon with the words "Dessins commandés à Rodin par M. Gallimard 1888." The original volume, formerly the property of the publisher Gallimard, who commissioned it, is now the property of the Musée Rodin. It has been published in facsimile editions, notably by The Limited Editions Club (London, 1940).

98. Using the pagination of the original volume and the sculpture numbers of the 1931 edition of the Grappe Musée Rodin catalogue, the six drawings based on sculpture are as follows. For *Le Guignon,* p. 35: *The Toilet of Venus,* no. 177; for *La Beauté,* p. 47: torso of *Meditation,* no. 154; for *L'Ideal* (not drawn in the same hatched style as the other five), p. 49: female figure from the couple *Avarice and Luxury,* no. 202; for *Remords posthume,* p. 78: a different view of *The Toilet of Venus;* for *Le Poison,* p. 106: *The Death of Adonis,* no. 252; for *Une Martyre,* p. 183: a forward view of the figure normally seen from the back in the group *Paolo and Francesca,* no. 206 (the same figure whose back-view is seen in one of the illustrations for *Enguerrande,* discussed below). See also Elsen's consideration of these illustrations in *Rodin's Gates of Hell.*

99. A variant version of the couple was reproduced in *Rodin,* catalogue of an exhibition, Villa Medici, Rome, 1967, Fig. 66; it is Musée Rodin no. 1913. I have seen in photograph another, apparently earlier version, entitled *L'Etoile,* which passed through a New York dealer's hands a few years ago. Further-

more, there is a "carbon-copy" transfer of the same couple in the Musée Rodin, no. 376, which bears the pen note "Victor Hugo," and also some minor pencil reworkings suggesting that Rodin envisioned putting Hugo's bearded profile on the head of the man in the couple.

100. The drawing for *La Béatrice*, p. 204, is a reworking of a figure of Dante from an earlier drawing, Musée Rodin no. 3768, pl. 3 of the Goupil volume, reproduced in Elsen's *Rodin's Gates of Hell*, pl. 10. The seated figure illustrating *Réversibilité*, is also found in Goupil, pl. 8. The winged figure illustrating *Tout Entière*, p. 85, is similar to studies from earlier gouached sheets in the Musée Rodin collection, especially no. 373.

101. Drawing no. 1986 in the Musée Rodin collection is the prototype for the illustration of a skeleton and woman dancing, used to accompany *Les Deux Bonnes Soeurs*, p. 199.

102. The figure derived from the *Eve* apparently refers to the scene in which the queen, Enguerrande, dries herself in a fisherman's cabin after a storm at sea. The other composition refers to the end of the poem; Gaëtan, the sculptor-prince, lies dead at the edge of a battlefield with Enguerrande.

103. The deluxe edition of Octave Mirbeau's *Le Jardin des Supplices* was published in Paris by Vollard, in 1902; it has twenty illustrations, reproduced from drawings, by the printer Clot. The edition of *Les Elégies Amoreuses d'Ovide*, translation by the Abbé Bazzin, was published by Editions Gonin, Paris, without date.

104. See Elsen's discussion in *Rodin's Gates of Hell*, p. 58. The figure seen from the back in the *Etudes* drypoint of 1881 (*Fig. 41*) anticipates this style quite closely, but its line purity may be the result of incompletion rather than intention.

105. The group is a tracing, in part, of a gouached drawing, Musée Rodin no. 2072, entitled *le temps* in the artist's hand.

106. The *Journal* of the Goncourts for December 29, 1887, records a conversation with Rodin: "He spoke to me about the illustrations of the poems of Baudelaire that he was in the process of executing for a connoisseur, and into which he would have liked to descend, in depth; but he wasn't able to do it, being too lightly paid—2,000 francs—and not being able to devote enough time to it. Also, for this book which will have no public life and which must remain enclosed in the bookcase of the connoisseur, he doesn't feel the spirit, the fire of an illustration project ordered by a publisher."

107. This letter is quoted by Elisabeth Chase Geissbuhler in *Rodin—Later Drawings* (Boston: Beacon Press, 1963), p. 2. Mrs. Geissbuhler points out that Judith Cladel dated the letter 1903.

108. Haavard Rostrup, "Les Dessins de Rodin," p. 216. In advancing my ideas for correction of this part of his chronology, I would like to express my thanks to Dr. Rostrup for the friendly assistance he extended to me in my research, and to stress the value of his essay, a pioneering work in the effort to order and understand Rodin's drawings.

109. Clément Janin, "Les Dessins de Rodin," pp. 286–87.

110. Charles Saunier, writing in *Les Arts Français* (February, 1918), p. 17, recollected: "An exhibition in a special pavilion, erected in the Place de l'Alma was, in 1900, a triumph for the artist. One remarked there a series of notations of gestures traced with a rapid line and heightened with wash, whose summary

formula contrasted with the rough drawings, so thickly worked up, of the preceding period."

111. These line reproductions appeared in Félicien Fagus's article "Discours sur la mission de Rodin," in *La Revue Blanche* (June 15, 1900); they were prepared by the graver Perrichon, who did many subsequent wood-block line reproductions of the later drawings.

112. In an anonymous article entitled "Rodin Dessinateur," *L'Echo de Paris* (May 10, 1899), the writer reported: "An exhibition dedicated to the work of Rodin has just opened in Brussels, at the art institution of the Avenue Toison d'Or. The author of *The Kiss* has exhibited in Brussels, besides a great number of sculptural works known in Paris, around a hundred original drawings which had never been out of his folios. These are, for the most part, curious studies from the studio, notations of the nude, taken in haste, to fix a pose of the model." The exhibition referred to showed in Amsterdam and Rotterdam as well.

113. Miss Cladel describes a "profusion" of drawings seen in Rodin's studio: "Nothing but contours, subtle or pressed, of a hair-like fineness, spreading out sometimes into beautiful thick lines, and, between them, the flow of a tint of aquarelle indicating the general tone of the skin. Hundreds of pages falling out of folios and, on each of them, an attitude, an action rather, seized by an eye as rapid as the movement itself." *Auguste Rodin pris sur la vie*, the book in which this appeared (p. 24), was only published in 1903, but a careful reading, taking into account the dates given by Miss Cladel, establishes the description as referring to 1898. On pp. 90–91 of the same book, there is a lengthy description of Rodin drawing from the model.

114. Maurice Guillemot, "Au Val-Meudon," *Le Journal* (August 17, 1898).

115. We have already cited the reproductions in the 1900 Félicien Fagus article. In the same year, *Art Journal*, LII, 13, published three rapid pencil drawings, and identified them as having been in the 1900 Rodin exhibition on the Place de l'Alma (my thanks to Victoria Thorson for this reference). The special issue of the *Revue des Beaux-Arts et des Lettres* (January 1, 1899), devoted to Rodin, published several line reproductions, on page 4 and page 9; these appear to be transitional works, in a style to be discussed below. Also in 1899, an album of lithographs entitled *Germinal*, edited by La Maison Moderne, included a reproduction of a very curious and highly simplified Rodin watercolor. The earliest reproduction of a late drawing known to me is that which figured in *L'Album des Peintres-Graveurs*, published by Vollard in 1897; I have been unable to locate a copy (only 100 impressions were pulled) to illustrate here, but the print is described by André Mellerio on page 18 of *La Lithographie Originale en Couleur*, Paris, 1898, as a reproduction traced by the printer Clot, of a drawing in "diluted sepia, in which, in an encircling line, the master sculptor encloses a curious and precise nude study of a woman."

116. Marx, "Cartons d'Artistes–Auguste Rodin," p. 299.

117. Gustave Geffroy, *La Vie Artistique*, 2nd vol. of a series (Paris: Dentu, 1893).

118. The original drawing for the print was published in 1899 among the *hors texte* plates in Léon Maillard's *Auguste Rodin, Statuaire*. I also know

the drawing through photograph, and can affirm that Maillard's reproduction is accurate. There is also a variant version of this group, in pen and sepia, in the Musée Rodin collection, no. 1964.

My thinking on this period of Rodin's draftsmanship has benefited from helpful discussions with Victoria Thorson.

119. Some writers whose credentials cannot be taken lightly would date the beginning of the late manner in the late 1880's. In the preface to a catalogue for an exhibition of Rodin drawings *Chez Devambez*, Paris, 1908, Louis Vauxcelles stated of the later drawings: "About twenty years ago, he had a model, with miraculous grace and flexibility, who gave him the most beautiful movements, the most sudden, the most original. He began to draw these thousands and thousands of times. Such is the origin of the present series." Rainer Maria Rilke, just having described the 1888 Baudelaire illustrations, wrote that: "The strange documents of the momentary and the unnoticeably passing originated at this time." (Rilke's 1903 essay, "Auguste Rodin," quoted in Elsen [ed.], *Readings*, p. 131.) These articles were both written a good deal after the period they describe, however, and the proximity of Marx's account, cited previously, to the time he describes lends it strong credibility. It is possible that Rodin began his drawing research into free movement in the late 1880's—the mention of a Javanese dancer series to be discussed below suggests that this is so—but that the late manner only reached definitive form toward the middle of the 1890's. Certainly there is no hint of it in the 1893 frontispiece (*Fig. 64*).

120. Léon Riotor, "Auguste Rodin," *Revue Populaire des Beaux-Arts* (April 8, 1899), remarked that Rodin had done an "innumerable sequence of portraits, and frontispieces for numerous works of his friends" (p. 216).

121. This letter from Rodin to Bourdelle was quoted and discussed by Elisabeth Chase Geissbuhler in *Rodin—Later Drawings*, p. 20. Rodin's characteristically aphoristic phrasing has been modified for clarity in our translation, and readers with special interest in the subject should consult the original French as quoted by Mrs. Geissbuhler.

122. In the 1920 edition of *Education de la memoire pittoresque*, p. 43, Lecoq describes special sessions in the country in which models were hired to move freely.

123. Dujardin-Beaumetz in Elsen (ed.), *Readings*, p. 164.

124. The Goncourt *Journal* for July 23, 1891, reads as follows: "In walking after dinner, Rodin spoke to me of his admiration for the Javanese dancers, of the sketches that he made of them, rapid sketches, not sufficiently penetrated with their exoticism and thereby having something of the antique. He spoke to me of a similar group of studies based on a Japanese village, transplanted to London, where there were likewise Japanese dancers. He finds our dances too jumpy, too broken, while in these dances, a succession of movements give birth to a snakelike effect, and undulation."

The Javanese dancers were undoubtedly those in the Javanese village at the 1889–90 Universal Exposition. In her article "Rodin et la danse," in *Art de France* (1963), Madame Cécile Goldscheider suggests that drawings of Javanese dancers can be identified among those commonly grouped under the rubric "Cambodian." The logic and support of her proposal are strong, but I feel that her system does not work in practice. For example, one drawing in Philadelphia that would be classified as Javanese under Madame Goldscheider's system clearly shows a costume peculiar to the Cambodian dancers. Furthermore, all evidence in other areas suggests that the large format and wash handling characteristic of all the sheets known as Cambodian dancers would not have been employed by Rodin in 1889–90.

125. Anthony Ludovici, *Personal Reminiscences of Auguste Rodin* (Philadelphia: Lippincott, 1926), pp. 138–139.

126. Rodin was quoted by Paul Gsell as saying: "One has accused . . . Delacroix of not knowing how to draw. The truth, on the contrary, is that his drawing is marvelously wedded to his color: like the latter, it is jerky, feverish, inspired; it has passages of hastiness, fits of passion; like the color, it is sometimes demented: and it is then that it is the most beautiful." (*L'Art, entretiens reunis par Paul Gsell* [Paris: Gallimard, 1967], p. 83.)

127. Aside from the visual evidence provided by comparisons and by comparative measurements, there is a solid documentary base for asserting Rodin's practice of tracing his later drawings. Clément Janin mentions it in the description quoted at the beginning of this section, and a letter from the wife of one of Rodin's secretaries describes the practice as well (see the discussion of *découpages* in the next section, Note 146). The first scholar to bring this matter to full light was Elisabeth Chase Geissbuhler. In *Rodin—Later Drawings*, p. 29, she recounted a description given to her by Bourdelle of Rodin tracing, and discussed the question specifically.

128. Dujardin-Beaumetz, in Elsen (ed.), *Readings*, p. 103. For a clear and well-documented account of the two stages of Rodin's work on the Balzac figure, see Jacques de Caso's "Balzac and Rodin in Rhode Island," *Bulletin of the Rhode Island School of Design* (May, 1966).

129. Camille Mauclair, "L'Art de M. Auguste Rodin," *Revue des Revues* (June 15, 1898), pp. 597–99, 607.

130. This paper is generally three to four thousandths of an inch thick, and usually shows a fine mechanical texture with transmitted light. A variant sheet size is the same height, but double the width; apparently the more common size was the result of slitting a larger sheet into halves. This basic paper type and general size is remarkably consistent in Rodin's later life-drawings.

131. In some cases, one finds a large band of wash across the lower part of the figure in Type II drawings. This wash is sometimes specifically construed as the ocean, with small boat added in a quick notation, giving the figure a colossal scale. In other cases, as in the *Nero*, wash additions may have been intended to cover parts of the drawing Rodin found less successful. Though the practice may seem to us to wreck the drawing rather than improve it, it is in accord with Rodin's penchant for eliminating all but the more satisfactory portions of sculptures after their enlargement, and his practice of covering with a drape those portions of the antique statues in his collection that he found less beautiful.

132. Drawings of Type I can be dated prior to 1900 by reproductions, notably those in the *Revue Blanche* of June 15, 1900 (*Fig. 62*); drawings of Type II were published in the 1902 edition of Mirbeau's *Jardin des Supplices* (*Fig. 68*); an article by Félicien Fagus, "Ses Collaborateurs," in *La Revue des Beaux-Arts et des Lettres*, January 1, 1899, makes it clear that these latter illustrations were already being prepared by the lithographer Clot at that date.

133. Gustave Coquiot, *Le Vrai Rodin* (Paris: Tallandier, 1913), pp. 159–60.

134. Paul Gsell, "Le Dessin et la Couleur," *La Revue* (October 1, 1910), p. 724.

135. A watercolor in the Boston Museum of Fine Arts, *La Toilette,* showing heavy stomping, entered the collection in 1907.

136. Describing a drawing session of 1898–99, in *Auguste Rodin pris sur la vie,* p. 91, Judith Cladel remarked: "One or two times the master passed his finger quickly over the line of the shoulders and over the curve of the hip, so that the touch would give it the indication that sight no longer perceived."

137. As the inscription on the drawing in Figure 78 states, it appeared in line reproduction on the cover of Judith Cladel's *Auguste Rodin, l'oeuvre et l'homme* (Brussels: Van Oest, 1908).

138. In the 1931 Musée Rodin catalogue, Grappe lists these *Studies of Movement* as numbers 442, 443, 444. Descharnes published a large number of the studies in color in *Rodin,* pp. 250–51.

139. Rodin saw the Cambodian dance group perform in Paris, and, intrigued, followed them to Marseilles, where they were among the star attractions of a large Colonial Exposition. He drew them during their practice sessions in the park of the Villa des Glycines. These facts, and Rodin's comments on the dancers, were recorded by George Bois in an article in the July 28, 1906, issue of *L'Illustration.* There is another account by Victor Frisch and Joseph Shipley, in *Auguste Rodin—A Biography* (New York: Stokes, 1938), pp. 164–68. This account would have us believe that the Cambodian troop consisted of 300 dancers (there were twenty), and that, at a lavishly described night garden party at Meudon (with full orchestra, and the Curies, Renoir, and Clemenceau in attendance), they danced nude for the artist. I regard this as a fabrication of the most irresponsible and reprehensible type. Much of this so-called biography is taken directly from the writings of others, but, in this case, there is not a whisper of support in the reports of anyone else associated with either Rodin or the Cambodian troop at this time.

140. The full text of Rodin's remarks on the Cambodian dancers, recorded by George Bois, is given and discussed by Elisabeth Geissbuhler in *Rodin—Later Drawings,* p. 38.

141. Grappe dates the statues 1911 in his 1931 catalogue. Descharnes dates them 1910 (see Note 138, above).

142. Leo Steinberg, from the Introduction to *Rodin—Sculptures and Drawings,* catalogue of an exhibition at the Slatkin Galleries, New York, 1963.

143. The drawing of the dancer in the National Gallery (*Fig. 77*) is dated 1909; however, a sketched notation made by Roger Marx in a 1908 catalogue now in the Philadelphia Museum of Art (*Dessins de Rodin,* chez Devambez, Paris, October–November, 1908) shows that the same pose appeared in a drawing entitled *Danse,* no. 115 of that exhibition.

144. Descharnes, *Rodin,* pp. 230–31.

145. The origins and makeup of the Chéruy collection are described, and one *découpage* published, in "Glimpses of Rodin," by Howard C. Rice, in the *Princeton University Library Chronicle,* XXVII, No. 1 (Autumn 1965). I am grateful to Mr. Rice for his help in researching the collection at Princeton.

146. In a letter to Howard C. Rice, Jr., dated September 24, 1965, Ger-

maine Chéruy suggested that Rodin may have cut the drawings out "in order to take them up and transfer them, which he did often—transferring (a drawing) in order to modify a line—at the window." The letter is now in the Chéruy collection at the Princeton University Library, Rare Books Division.

147. Ludovici, *Personal Reminiscences of Auguste Rodin*, pp. 133–34.

148. The correspondence between Rodin and Bourdelle on this matter is quoted and discussed by Elisabeth Chase Geissbuhler in *Rodin—Later Drawings,* pp. 1–2, 51–53, 85.

149. Paul Gsell quotes Rodin as follows: "One imagines that a drawing can be beautiful in and of itself. It is so only by virtue of the truths, the feeling that it communicates." And further: "There is no good style except that which makes itself forgotten in order to concentrate all the attention of the viewer on the subject dealt with, on the emotion rendered." (*L'Art, entretiens avec Rodin* [Paris: Gallimard, 1967], p. 78.)

150. A letter from Rodin to Bourdelle, quoted by Elisabeth Chase Geissbuhler in *Rodin—Later Drawings*, p. 20.

151. Charles Quentin, "Rodin," *The Art Journal* (July 1898), p. 194.

Symbolism and Conservatism in Rodin's Late Drawings

VICTORIA THORSON

TWO NATURES OF woman particularly fascinated Rodin: the erotic and the spiritual. In his late drawings (1900–1917),[1] he dramatized the erotic by drawing a naked woman with her legs spread apart, her hands pressing her breasts together, or flaunting her body with arms behind her head. He symbolized her spiritual nature by characterizing her as Venus, a Greek vase, a butterfly, or the Sun. Rodin once said:

> Among so many expressions of humanity . . . which I was given to admire, there are two especially with which I worked at length, and which I seem still to see: two Italian girls, one dark, the other blonde. They were sisters, and both were the perfection of absolutely opposite natures. One was superb in her savage strength. The other had that sovereign beauty which all poets have sung. The dark one had sunburned skin, warm, with the bronze reflections of women of sunny lands; her movements were quick and feline, with the lissomeness and grace of a panther. . . . The other sister was marvelously beautiful, beautiful as Venus, as Apollo; her skin, white and dewy. . . . All over her body she had little downy hairs which, in daylight, surrounded her with gilded radiance; you would have said that she was dressed in light.[2]

Rays of light, perhaps symbolizing spiritual radiance, are represented in several drawings by straight lines, about an inch apart, surrounding the body of the female model. On one drawing, which Rodin inscribed "haut aube," he also sketched a circle behind the model's torso

121

as an emblem of the sun.[3] Three drawings, *The Rising Sun* (*Fig. 92*), *The Afternoon Sun*, and *The Setting Sun* (*Color Plate III*), exhibited at the Stieglitz Photo-Secession Gallery in 1910,[4] were designated the "Sun Series" in the Gallery's magazine.[5] Rodin wrote "quittant la terre" on *The Rising Sun*, in which a model, rising from the ground on one foot, represents the morning sun. In *The Setting Sun*, Rodin drew the kneeling model with her head bent toward the earth and later inscribed it "bas soleil."

These were originally simple figure studies of a model whose rising and falling movements subsequently reminded Rodin of the sun. Drawing the model and later giving it a particular significance was characteristic of the artist in his late period (though he had sometimes returned in this fashion to earlier drawings). In his late drawings, Rodin concentrated on the model and drew her contours without looking down at his pencil, capturing her spontaneous gesture without preconceived meaning or conscious style.

> . . . he tries . . . to represent the principal volume of a figure. . . . he produces hundreds and hundreds of drawings. Those which he considers good, that is, significant, are kept. He takes them for a work as simple as the first: he limits himself to fill in the contour which he has sketched . . . with a sort of terra cotta color which suffices for him to represent the figure's volume. . . . When the drawings are finished in the form which was described, he finds that they take on unforseen and multiple significances. . . .[6]

By inscribing "le soleil" on a drawing, Rodin made the study of a live model into a symbolic image, in keeping with Rodin's Symbolist idea that "lines and colors are only to us the symbols of hidden realities."[7] Other inscriptions, like the mythological "Psyché" or the literary "Neron,"[8] ennobled the model's image and revealed Rodin's conservative attitude that a common name like "head" vulgarized a work.[9] Rodin also transformed the sketch of the model into symbolic or conservative motifs by formal pictorial means. A line drawing might be covered with layers of wash, shading, or lines of emphasis and characterization, or embellished with forms such as a snake.

In the Sun Series, by first drawing the model and later interpreting her form, Rodin transformed the traditional allegory of the Sun, always represented by a male figure in mythology, into a female figure surrounded by rays. Rodin associated light or radiance with woman's ethereal beauty or spiritual nature: "The dazzling splendor revealed to the artist by the model that divests herself of her clothes has the effect of the sun piercing the clouds. Venus, Eve, these are feeble terms to express the beauty of woman."[10]

Rodin, the conservative who said, "I judged in effect as my antique predecessors, that the body is the only true dress of the soul, that which transmits its radiance,"[11] may have also conceived of his sun symbols as classical figures of women crowned with rays, perhaps associated with specific antique sculpture.[12]

The women of the Sun Series have an aloof, spiritual beauty and lack of sexuality conveyed by means of athletic gestures and stylistic refinements. When he traced their figures from previous sketches, Rodin centered the compositions and smoothed and abstracted details of the model's body to express a heightened spiritual quality.

Not all late drawings symbolizing man's spiritual nature were refined, however, as Rodin actually exploited the results of chance in some late drawings. In *Figure Drawing* (*Fig. 93*) he added wings to a sketch of a moving model, transforming the figure into a butterfly, a common symbol of the human spirit. The wings may have been suggested by the accidental shape of the watercolor pools behind the figure, which Rodin accentuated slightly with pencil. (He repeated the butterfly motif created out of accidental splashes of watercolor in another late drawing now in the Musée Rodin in Paris, no. 4536.)

In *Figure Drawing,* the subject is a hermaphrodite, a bisexual creature who appears occasionally in Rodin's drawings[13] but not in his sculpture. Rodin may have sketched breasts on top of a previously drawn male figure[14] to create a hermaphroditic Eros, similar to the bisexual representations of the winged god in Greek sculptures in the Louvre,[15] or he may have intended to change the sex of the male figure to female by adding breasts, the reverse of the change in the drawing *Nero* (*Fig. 94*) where a sketch of a female model was later changed into an image of the emperor Nero.

The butterfly symbol of Figure 93 recurs in another drawing depicting a woman dancing with veils spread behind her like butterfly wings (*Fig. 95*). Inscribed "le papillon" by Rodin, the drawing may portray the dancer Loie Fuller as she performed the "Dance of the Butterfly" wearing wings of wired veil.[16] The wings and light movements transformed her dancing body into a butterfly—the symbol of the human spirit.

Although Rodin usually recorded the model's natural gesture first and later discovered a significance in what he had drawn, he sometimes posed models to illustrate a preconceived idea. He told Renoir: "The Russians are wonderful dancers. I got one of them to pose on top of a column—one leg bent back and arms stretched upward. I was trying to make a genie rising into flight."[17]

In *Nude with Draperies* (*Fig. 74*) the model's upper body relates closely to classical portrayals of Venus.[18] Even in his late drawing, Rodin may have continued an academic practice of posing the live model after a classical statue.[19] However, Rodin's models were generally unprofessional and therefore unfamiliar with the standard classical poses.[20] Rodin may have suggested the classical pose to her, just as he asked the Russian

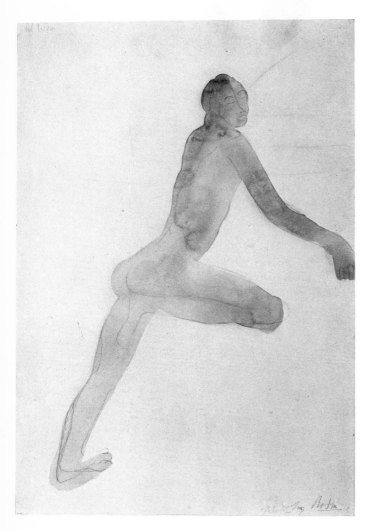

92. *The Rising Sun (Quittant la terre)*, c. 1900–1905. Sun Series. Lead pencil, watercolor wash. 19 x 12½ inches. Courtesy of The Art Institute of Chicago. The Alfred Stieglitz Collection.

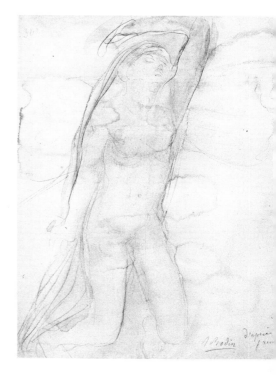

93. *Figure Drawing*, 1900–1917. Lead pencil, watercolor wash. 12⅝ x 9½ inches. Collection of Mrs. Patience Smith Echols, Baltimore. On indefinite loan to The Baltimore Museum of Art.

94. *Nero*, c. 1900–1905. Lead pencil, watercolor wash, gouache. 12¹³⁄₁₆ x 9⅞ inches. The Metropolitan Museum of Art, New York. Kennedy Fund, 1910.

95. *Sketch of Dancing Figure with Draperies*, 1900–1917. Lead pencil, watercolor wash. 10⅝ x 6⅛ inches. Fogg Art Museum, Harvard University, Cambridge, Massachusetts.

dancer to pose on top of a column. In any case, by drawing this pose in profile and adding drapery, arranged as if draped over an antique vase, Rodin emphasized its classical prototype.

For Rodin, the figure of Venus he drew in *Nude with Draperies* meant more than the repetition of an art-school exercise. In contrast to many academic artists who could scarcely see life in a Greek statue, Rodin saw the classical statue and the living model simultaneously. The image of Venus in this drawing exists in the classical pose of the upper body, and a living form with lifelike movement is reflected in the legs. Rodin saw the classical statue of the *Venus de Milo* as a real woman, based on a direct observation of nature rather than an idealization.[21] Therefore, late drawings inscribed with names of classical goddesses or reflecting antique poses may be interpreted as the spiritual nature of woman as it was manifested in a Greek statue.

Rodin also continued an academic tradition when he drew a woman's torso in the shape of a Greek vase (*Figs. 80 and 96*), following a common analogy that Matisse related to his students in 1908: "This pelvis fits into the thigh and suggests an amphora!"[22] In Rodin's words: "When I draw the body of a woman I rediscover the form of the beautiful Greek vases."[23] The substantial number of Greek-vase drawings, including those done for the only book illustrations he undertook after 1900,[24] suggest that the analogy had a personal meaning for Rodin beyond the repetition of an academic metaphor.

A clue to this personal meaning probably lies in the inscription on one of the vase drawings (*Fig. 96*): "naissance du vase grec" ("origin of the Greek vase"). By this, Rodin meant that the Greeks derived their forms from nature, the amphora originating from the form of a woman's torso. Rodin formalized the relationship between the shape of the vase and a woman's torso to develop his symbol. First, he chose a model with what he believed were Greek proportions: "equal width of shoulders and hips . . . [in contrast to] many French women . . . [whose] hips are strongly developed and the shoulders are narrower."[25] All the models represented in the Greek vase drawings have equally wide shoulders and hips.

Second, Rodin had the model pose frontally or from the back, either seated or kneeling, so that the form of the torso predominated. In Figures 80 and 96 the model is in frontal position, while in another Greek vase drawing, in the Philadelphia Museum of Art, the model is viewed from the back.[26] Rodin said: "At another time it [the human body] is an urn. I have often asked a model to sit on the ground with her back to me, her arms and legs gathered in front of her. In this position the back, which tapers to the waist and swells at the hips, appears like a vase of exquisite outline."[27]

Finally, Rodin emphasized the form of the torso, by omitting the head in some examples[28] and by abstracting the form in subsequent repetitions, so that it became a complete aesthetic unit. The Greek-vase drawings express and support Rodin's revolutionary view that a fragment of nature like the torso, can be the origin of a complete aesthetic form, like the vase. Many partial figures in his sculpture represent the same idea.[29]

In strong contrast to the refined, formalized movements of the models in the spiritual sun, Venus, and Greek-vase drawings are the erotic poses suggestive of woman's sexual nature that Rodin isolated and repeated in his drawings and sculptures.

The woman displaying her body with one or both arms behind her head is the classic expression of seduction, derived from Greek art and incorporated into the "Beauty" pose of the nineteenth-century ateliers. Rodin's choice of this gesture may reflect his occasional use of academic poses or simply the model's natural way of stretching (*Fig. 97*) or resting (*Fig. 98*). In any case, if the model appeared erotic in this pose, Rodin might call her image "temptress," as in the drawings and sculptures of the *Temptation of St. Anthony*,[30] or "bacchante"[31] or simply leave the work untitled. Two untitled works, the sculpture *Torso of Adèle*[32] and the drawing *Reclining Female Nude* (*Fig. 98*) both show a naked woman in this pose with her torso arched back seductively and her breasts proffered.

A more artistically unusual erotic gesture of a woman pressing her breasts together with her hands is found in a number of Rodin's late drawings (*Figs. 99 and 100*). Although most contemporary critics only alluded generally to the sexual gestures in Rodin's drawings (the "symbolization of passion," for example[33]) Louis Lumet, in 1908, focused on the image of *Cleopatra* pressing her breasts together with her hands. "Among others, you admire *Cleopatra* . . . female-queen with frail haunches, her hands contracting her breasts (*les mains crispée aux seins*), seceding from love and crying again for love. There is here an extraordinary sexual appetite, ardent, never satisfied."[34] Lumet's description of *Cleopatra* closely relates to the drawing *Egypte* (*Fig. 100*)[35] where the figure has the same frail hips, presses her breasts together with her hands, and is given a similar Egyptian title. If Lumet correctly interpreted *Cleopatra's* gesture,[36] then *Egypte* and other drawings with this pose symbolize a woman's unsatisfied sexual desire at the moment when passion subsides and new desire arises.

A third sexual image is the naked woman with her legs spread apart, exposing her sexual organs (*Figs. 83, 101, and 139*). These images were drawn and exhibited during the latter part of Rodin's life[37] and were considered by his contemporaries as among his most erotic works.[38] The increased eroticism in Rodin's work seems to correspond to his less inhibited attitude toward women in later life: "At age twenty, I slighted them; I did not know that at seventy I would love them. I had scorned them because I was timid."[39]

96. *The Origin of the Greek Vase*, 1900–1913. Lead pencil, watercolor wash. 19⅜ x 12⅝ inches. The Metropolitan Museum of Art, New York. Gift of Thomas F. Ryan, 1913.

97. *Seated Female Nude*, c. 1900. Lead pencil. 12⁵⁄₁₆ x 7¾ inches. Musée Rodin, Paris (no. 798). Photograph by Adelys.

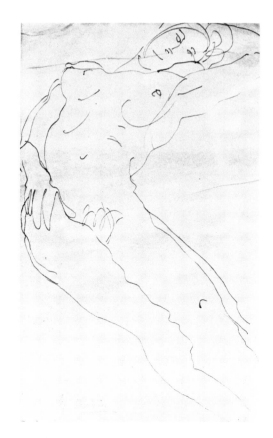

98. *Reclining Female Nude*, c. 1900. Pen and ink. 12 x 7⅝ inches. Collection of Mr. and Mrs. Laurence Brunswick, Jr., Rydal, Pennsylvania.

99. *Standing Female Nude, Squeezing Breasts Together*, c. 1900. Pen and ink, gouache. 14 x 9¼ inches. Rodin Museum, Philadelphia Museum of Art.

100. *Egypte*, 1900–1908. Lead pencil, watercolor wash. 19¼ x 12¼ inches. Collection of Joanna T. Steichen, West Redding, Connecticut.

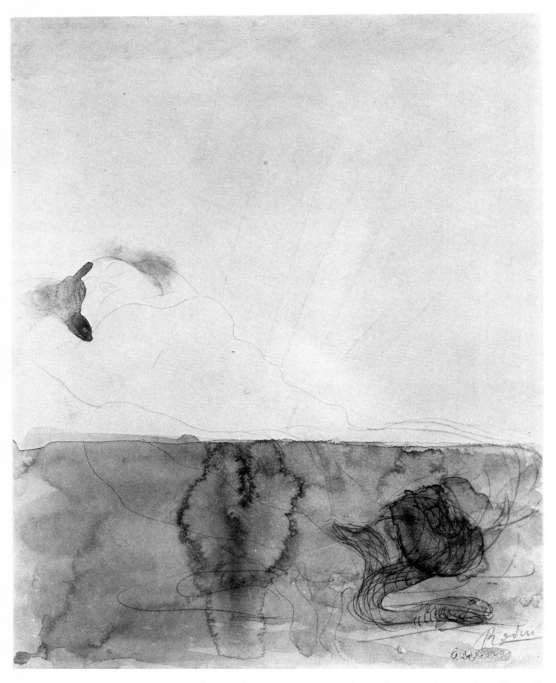

101. *Woman with a Snake*, c. 1900–1905. Lead pencil, watercolor wash. 12⅝ x 9¾ inches. Collection, The Museum of Modern Art, New York. Gift of Mr. and Mrs. Patrick Dinehart.

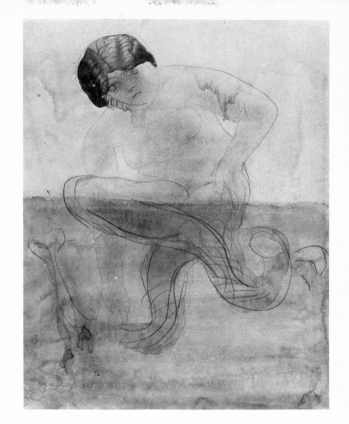

102. *The Mermaid*, c. 1900–1905. Lead pencil, watercolor wash. 13⅛ x 10½ inches. Museum of Art, Rhode Island School of Design, Providence.

103. *Witches' Sabbath (Sabbat)*, 1880–90. Lead pencil, watercolor wash. 12¾ x 9¾ inches. The Metropolitan Museum of Art, New York. Gift of Georgia O'Keeffe, 1965.

The pose of women with their legs apart appears earlier in sculptures related to *The Gates of Hell* project; in this tragic context the erotic pose is interpreted as anguished sexual frustration, called "the most tragic sensuality"[40] and "mournful lust"[41] by contemporary critics. Later, about 1900, in a sculpture called *Study: Female Torso*[42] and in his late drawings of naked women with their legs spread apart, Rodin omitted the tragic overtone and concentrated unequivocally on sex. In the fragment sculpture *Study: Female Torso* and in *Nude Figure* (*Fig. 139*) Rodin omitted the lower legs to focus on the vagina and breasts, which, in the drawing, he further accentuated with heavy black lines.

Beneath the smooth traced image of a naked woman with her legs spread apart, Rodin scribbled a snake in *Woman with a Snake* (*Fig. 101*). The nude woman appears to be a sun symbol with light rays surrounding her upper torso in a fashion recalling the Sun Series. The blue-black wash across her lower torso may symbolize the sea, as in *The Mermaid* (*Fig. 102*), where Rodin transformed the image of a seated model into a two-tailed siren by adding fish tails to both legs and a wash representing the sea over her lower body. Since Rodin added the snake over the wash in Figure 101, he may have first conceived of the composition without the snake, as a sunset or sunrise, as in the drawing *Sun on Sea*[43] and in his words: "Woman enters by her head and upper body into the realm of sleep . . . she plunges in the charming lake of sleep as the sun plunges into the sea."[44]

Another interpretation (perhaps a subsequent one) is suggested by the fact that Rodin inscribed "l'aube retour du sabbat" ("return from the Sabbath at dawn") on an earlier drawing (*Fig. 91*).[45] (The revelers return at dawn from the feast of the Witches' Sabbath.) The sun in *Woman with a Snake* may refer to this time of day, and the snake may symbolize intercourse at the orgy of the Sabbath, as it probably does in Louis Boulanger's drawing *La Ronde du Sabbat*,[46] one of several nineteenth-century illustrations of the Sabbath that Rodin may have known.

In earlier drawings inscribed "sabbat," Rodin symbolized intercourse by showing the ride of the Sabbath—a broom (*Fig. 103*), centaur (*Fig. 91*), or a hybrid snake-centaur (*Fig. 104*) is placed between the spread legs of a naked woman as her steed or sexual partner. The similarity of the phallic steed between the rider's legs with the snake just beneath the woman's crotch in *Woman with a Snake* suggests the same symbolism of intercourse (though perhaps not at the orgy of the Sabbath).

Another source for the images in *Woman with a Snake* may have been the allegory of Lust, accompanied by her attribute the snake, known to Rodin from his study of medieval cathedrals. Rodin may also have been influenced by the engravings of Félicien Rops,[47] a literary Symbolist whom Rodin knew and admired. Rodin's conception, however, is closer to that of the intuitive and personal Symbolist Odilon Redon.

Redon's dual image of a snake superimposed on the lower body of a woman suggests, rather than directly illustrates a passage in Flaubert's *Temptation of St. Anthony* where the temptress Lust merges with Death.[48] The meaning in Rodin's *Woman with a Snake* is similarly allusive; the drawing reveals an intuitive Symbolist mind like Redon's, whose symbols cannot be understood by relating them to outside sources. At best, the sources indicate that the images in *Woman with a Snake* may symbolize Lust rather than represent intercourse at the orgy of the Sabbath.

The symbolic images of *Woman with a Snake* are made even more complex by their mixed modes of drawing. Beneath the woman's body described by a finely-spun, caressing line, Rodin scribbled a snake with the frenzy of an attack, simulating a possible sexual involvement with the image of the model seen in another late drawing, the *Satyress* (*Fig. 83*). Here, Rodin scribbled dark lines over the sketch of a model's grossly heavy and voluptuous body to transform her legs into the hairy hooved limbs of a satyress, echoing his attitude: "Art is nothing else but a sensual voluptuousness. It is only a derivative [of] the power of loving. By creating, the artist deceives his [generative] instinct. . . . By the lines, the forms, the color he expresses his idolatry. He caresses her, he adorns her with the most seductive charms. He is the lover. She is the lover."[49] Thus, if the *Woman with a Snake* symbolizes lust or intercourse, the frenetically scribbled snake implies a sexual assault on the image of the model.

This attack is subdued, however, in comparison with the earlier "black-period" drawing (*Fig. 103*), where a broom penetrates deeply into the woman's body suggesting violent, perhaps brutal intercourse. The explicit violence of the earlier drawing typifies the aggressive physical struggles of many "black-period" drawings (*Fig. 105*) and shows a greater clarity and directness associated with nineteenth-century Romantic art. By contrast, the suggested intercourse in *Woman with a Snake* and the quiet embraces of lesbian lovers (*Fig. 106*) are closer to the ambiguities of intuitive Symbolism. The themes of both the "black-period" and late Symbolist drawings show that Rodin remained an artist of fantasy throughout his life.

Rodin also retained many conservative ideas in his later years. Classical poses (*Fig. 74*), academic titles (*Apotheosis* and *Vanquished*[50]), and literary and mythological inscriptions ("Neron" and "Psyché") are vestiges of nineteenth-century conservatism in Rodin's drawings that also appear in his sculpture. According to one nineteenth-century critic, ". . . the superior forms of his art are history and allegory. For poetic history, M. Rodin used the motif of the *Kiss* . . . for legendary history . . . *The Burghers of Calais*."[51]

Most of Rodin's late drawings, however, lie somewhere between an exclusively Symbolist or conservative orientation. Rodin started with the

104. *Witches' Sabbath (Le Sabbat),*
c. 1883. Pen and ink, gouache. 5¾ x
7½ inches. Courtesy of The Art Institute of Chicago. Gift of Robert Al-
lerton.

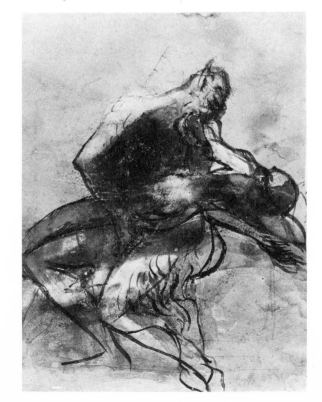

105. *Satyr and Nymph,* c. 1883. Pen
and ink, ink wash, gouache. 4⅞ x
3⅜ inches. Rodin Museum, Philadelphia Museum of Art. Given by Jules
Mastbaum.

premise, taken from heroic art, that a gesture or movement of the body could symbolize a human attitude. However, Rodin departed from academic ideas when he drew the model's natural gestures with his new techniques. He once said that the art of his friend Puvis de Chavannes inspired one "to feel oneself capable of noble deeds."[52] Similarly, Rodin continued the heroic tradition while developing new methods of expression that relate him to the Symbolists of his period.

106. *The Duo*, c. 1900. Lead pencil. 12¼ x 7½ inches. Collection of Mr. Martin Revson, New York.

NOTES

1. The date 1900 for the beginning of the mature period of Rodin's late drawing style is approximate. See the essay on chronology by Kirk Varnedoe.

2. H. E. C. Dujardin-Beaumetz, "Rodin's Reflections on Art," in Albert Elsen (ed.), *Auguste Rodin: Readings on His Life and Work* (Englewood Cliffs, N.J.: Prentice-Hall, 1965), pp. 164–65.

3. Musée Rodin, Paris, no. 4868.

4. *Exhibition of Drawings by Auguste Rodin*, catalogue of an exhibition at the Photo-Secession Gallery, New York, March 31–April 16, 1910. *The Rising Sun*, no. 26 on the one-page exhibition checklist, *The Afternoon Sun*, no. 27, and *The Setting Sun*, no. 28, comprise the Sun Series. There is a copy of the exhibition checklist in The Metropolitan Museum of Art, New York.

5. *Camera Work* (magazine of the Alfred Stieglitz Photo-Secession Gallery), Nos. 34–35 (April–July, 1911), p. 61.

6. Gustave Geffroy, *La Vie Artistique* (Paris: H. Floury, VII, 1901), pp. 259–60. For a more complete description of Rodin's late drawing style see Kirk Varnedoe's essay.

7. Paul Gsell, *Art by Auguste Rodin* (London: Hodder & Stoughton, 1912), p. 190. For Rodin as a Symbolist see also Arthur Symons, *From Toulouse-Lautrec to Rodin* (London: John Lane the Bodley Head, 1929).

8. The drawing inscribed "Neron" (*Fig. 94*) probably re-creates the image of the Emperor Nero's arms steeped in blood, an important symbolic image in Racine's play *Britannicus*; Rodin showed his familiarity with the play and his admiration for Racine's characterization of Nero in a discussion with Paul Gsell (Gsell, *Art by Auguste Rodin*, p. 44).

9. Ambroise Vollard, *Auguste Renoir* (Paris: Editions G. Crés, 1920), p. 190.

10. Judith Cladel, *Rodin, the Man and His Art*, S. K. Star, trans. (New York: The Century Co., 1917), p. 143.

11. Paul Gsell, "Chez Rodin," *L'Art et les artistes* (February, 1907) p. 410.

12. See the commemorative monument to Julia Victorina, in which a girl's head is surrounded by rays symbolizing the sun. *Encyclopedie photographique de l'art* (Musée National du Louvre, Editions Tel, 1935), III, 288.

13. *Catalogue des tableaux modernes formant la collection de M. Jacques Zubaloff*, Galerie Georges Petit, Paris, June 16–17, 1927, p. 79, *Étude pour une tentation de Saint Antoine*.

14. The model in *Figure Drawing* probably was a man, judging from the Adam's apple, the straight lines of the body, the muscles of the shoulders, the biceps, and the natural way the male genitals move with the body; the half circles of the breasts appear to be drawn over the straight lines of the chest.

15. *Encyclopédie photographic de l'art*, II, 209, 229, and 231.

16. Loie Fuller, *Fifteen Years of a Dancer's Life* (London: Herbert Jenkins, 1913), pp. 143 and 181.

17. Vollard, *Auguste Renoir*, p. 250.

18. The head, torso and left arm are similar to the *Venus Callipyge* in the National Museum of Naples, which is reproduced in Rodin's article "A la Venus de Milo," *L'Art et les artistes* (March, 1914), p. 103. See also *Encyclopédie photographic de l'art*, II, 176, *Venus Genetrix*, and II, 186, *Venus d'Arles*.

19. Albert Boime, *The Academy and French Painting in the Nineteenth Century* (New York: Phaidon, 1970), pp. 22-36. This practice was intended to make easier the student's transition from sketching casts of Greek statues to drawing the live model. The Greek poses were also chosen for their simplicity. While drawing from the cast and the live model, the student was instructed to pay attention to halftones of light. In his article "A la Venus de Milo," Rodin frequently mentioned the beauty and importance of the halftones (*demi-teintes*), reflecting the importance to him of the academic training. Rodin continued to use halftones, produced by the *estompe* technique, in many late drawings (*Fig. 80*).

20. Dujardin-Beaumetz in Elsen (ed.), *Readings*, p. 166. One of several references to his unprofessional models is Rodin's description of an Italian peasant who posed for the sculpture *St. John the Baptist*.

21. "A la Venus de Milo," p. 92; Rodin wrote, "tu es Femme, et c'est là ta gloire."

22. Sarah Stein, "Appendix A: Matisse Speaks to His Students, 1908," in Alfred H. Barr, Jr., *Matisse* (New York: The Museum of Modern Art, 1966), p. 550.

23. Cladel, *Rodin*, p. 247.

24. *Les Elégies Amoureuses d'Ovide*, translated into French by the Abbé Bazzin, decorations by A. Rodin, preface by Georges Grappe (Paris: Philippe Gonin, 1935), pl. 31. (The drawings were executed "vers 1900," according to Grappe.) Also Octave Mirbeau, *Le Jardin des Supplices*, with twenty compositions by Auguste Rodin (Paris: Ambroise Vollard, 1902), frontispiece.

25. Gsell, *Art by Auguste Rodin*, p. 118.

26. Philadelphia Museum of Art, no. F 1929-7-152.

27. Gsell, *Art by Auguste Rodin*, p. 122.

28. Mirbeau, *Le Jardin des Supplices*, frontispiece.

29. Albert Elsen, *The Partial Figure in Modern Sculpture from Rodin to 1969*, catalogue of an exhibition at The Baltimore Museum of Art, Baltimore, Maryland, December 2, 1969–February 1, 1970, pp. 16–28.

30. Gustave Coquiot, *Rodin à l'Hôtel de Biron et à Meudon* (Paris: Librairie Ollendorff, 1917), p. 79 drawing of the *Temptation of St. Anthony*. Also, California Palace of the Legion of Honor, plaster of the *Temptation of St. Anthony*.

31. Louis Vauxcelles, "Les Dessins de Rodin," introduction and catalogue of *Exposition de dessins d'Auguste Rodin*, Chez Devambez, Paris, October 19–November 5, 1908, no. 1, *Bacchante*. In his annotated catalogue of the exhibition, Roger Marx drew a small sketch of no. 1 in the catalogue opposite the title *Bacchante*, showing a standing woman with one arm behind her head. (A copy of the annotated catalogue is located in the Philadelphia Museum of Art.) Also Gustave Geffroy, "Auguste Rodin," catalogue of *Exposition Claude Monet–A. Rodin*, Galerie Georges Petit, Paris, 1889, p. 31. Geffroy describes a sculpture of a fauness: "hands tied behind her head, a febrile gesture of seduction and teasing." The fauness, bacchante, and satyress (the title of a

sculpture listed as no. 14 in the catalogue) are symbols for the sexual nature of woman.

32. Albert Elsen, *Rodin* (New York: The Museum of Modern Art, 1967), p. 183, illustrated. In *Torso of Adèle,* though the woman's arm is in front of her head, the pose is a variation of the arm behind the head seduction pose.

33. Gustave Geffroy "The Sculptor Rodin," *Art and Letters,* III (1889), p. 301.

34. Louis Lumet, "Les Dessins d'Auguste Rodin," *Les Arts Français* (1918), p. 32.

35. *Les Dessins de Rodin,* catalogue of an exhibition at the Bernheim-Jeune Gallery, Paris, October 1907. The catalogue lists the title *Cleopatre* (no. 4), probably the drawing described by Louis Lumet in his review of the exhibition in *Les Arts Français* (1918), and the title *Egypte* (no. 52), possibly the drawing inscribed "Egypte" in the collection of Mrs. Edward Steichen, West Redding, Connecticut.

36. Since Lumet understood the pose it may have been known and used by other artists. In Rodin's work, another drawing with the pose was published in *L'Art et les artistes* (1914), p. 74, and similar poses appear both in drawings and sculptures (though there are no sculptures with this exact pose). A woman presses her breasts with her arms and a woman lifts her breasts with her hands in two drawings published in 1900 *(La Revue Blanche,* [June 15,], p. 243). A woman touches her breast with one hand in the sculptures *Crouching Woman* (Elsen, *Rodin,* p. 58, illustrated) and *Muse* (also called *Inner Voice*) (Elsen, *Rodin,* p. 209, illustrated).

37. *Exhibition of Drawings by Auguste Rodin,* Photo-Secession, no. 1, *Sabbat (Fig. 103),* drawing dated 1880–90 and exhibited in 1910. Also, Vauxcelles, "Les Dessins de Rodin," no. 76, *Tombée dans l'eau.* The drawing is sketched in Roger Marx's annotated catalogue showing the spread-legs pose.

38. Félicien Fagus, "Cinquante Lettres," *Le Divan* (1934–35), p. 242.

39. Mme. Aurel, "Rodin et la femme, notes inédites de Rodin," *Grande Revue* (December, 1917), p. 253.

40. Fagus, "Cinquante Lettres," p. 242; "la plus tragique sensualité."

41. Gustave Geffroy, *La Vie Artistique* (Paris: E. Dentu, 1893), II; "la luxure triste."

42. Elsen, *Rodin,* p. 150, illustrated.

43. *Les Dessins de Rodin,* Bernheim-Jeune Gallery, no. 141, *Le Soleil dans la mer.*

44. Aurel, "Rodin et la femme," p. 240.

45. Drawings subsequently referred to as "earlier" drawings in this article are from Rodin's "black-drawing" period. See article by Kirk Varnedoe on chronology for date.

46. Albert Elsen, "Rodin's 'La Ronde'," *Burlington Magazine* (June, 1965), pl. 16, illustrated.

47. Jean Paul Dubray, *Félicien Rops* (Paris: Editions Marcel Seheur, 1928), p.14. In *Le Pécher mortel* by Rops, a snake attacks the breast and vagina of a naked woman in a manner similar to many medieval depictions of Lust.

48. Richard Sydney Overstreet, "Death Imagery in Symbolist Painting" (unpublished master's thesis) University of California at Berkeley, September,

1960). The thesis includes a good discussion of Redon's "snake-woman" symbol, very briefly summarized here.

49. Paul Gsell (Introduction), *Dix Dessins Inédites par Auguste Rodin* (Paris: Albert Besnard, 1921), p. 9.

50. *Les Dessins de Rodin*, Bernheim-Jeune, no. 115 *Apothéose*, and no. 123, *Vaincue*. Though who gave the drawings their titles is not known, it is probable that Rodin approved of the title, whether or not he wrote them, for the exhibition was held with his cooperation.

51. Gustave Larroumet, "Rodin," *Supplement du Figaro*, January 12, 1895.

52. Gsell, *Art by Auguste Rodin*, p. 58.

Preliminary Notes on Rodin's Architectural Drawings

ELISABETH CHASE GEISSBUHLER

WHEN THE ENEMY has penetrated behind our lines we can only resist from within and with native arms. So in the present effort to rout from the ranks of Rodin's true drawings the forgeries that have infiltrated private collections, museums, and publications of two continents, our sound policy would seem to muster his drawings that cannot be doubted.

With but two exceptions, forgers have caused doubt to be cast on all forms and phases of Rodin's mature work. The exceptions are his monuments and his architectural drawings. Small, frail and, at first glance, unimpressive, these architectural drawings have a history that is entirely without incident. They have not only never been forged, they have never been evaluated. In this latter, they are even distinguished from Rodin's written architectural sketches, which, of course, make identical statements, only in a different language, since both were born of the same emotion—Rodin's admiration for the art of his ancestors. For the written architectural notes have been endlessly quoted, and, whether favorably or unfavorably judged, at least very frequently written about. Such contrary circumstances attending one consistent concern seem to have sprung originally from Rodin's own attitude toward his architectural drawings.[1]

There would, no doubt, have been market enough for forgeries of the architectural drawings had Rodin shown them during the first years of the twentieth century. At that time his written notes were appearing in every book and article of the many written about him. Then, too,

Rodin himself began answering questionnaires, sending letters to editors and short articles to newspapers and magazines. So for any forgeries there might have been a market at least as good as for any paper that bore his name. But none of his architectural drawings was signed or dated. This was to be expected, as it was Rodin's habit to sign and sometimes to date his life drawings only when he sold or exhibited them, and no architectural drawings were exhibited, still less offered for sale. Only a group of their reproductions, apparently the trial sheets that he approved as illustrations for his book, do have his signature (these are now at the Rodin Museum in Philadelphia).

Most people first learned of the existence of these drawings of architecture when 100 appeared a few months before the outbreak of World War I as illustrations for Rodin's only book: *Les Cathédrales de France*.[2] That book, and particularly its illustrations, have suffered severely from unavailability: In France, the text was last printed in 1953, and the illustrations have not been published there since 1914.[3] Thus, the architectural drawings were the last phase of Rodin's art to come before the public and the first to disappear. Yet, by his word, he had been studying old French architecture since 1865, and we know his written and graphic notes on that subject were still being made in 1913.

In his *North American Review* article, Rodin said:

> When I had rid myself of the prejudice of my environment and dared to look with my own eyes, at about age twenty-five, although to some extent by the time I was twenty, only then did I begin to make a special study of Gothic art. . . . Wherever I went I made it a rule to visit all the churches . . . and I remember that the spires and various parts of these gave me exquisite joy.[4]

Any such "special study" by Rodin, we dare to affirm, included from the beginning many sketches and probably detailed drawings of whatever gave him joy. So we believe it is only by accident if no drawings and no documents have survived that are earlier than his letter of 1875 to Rose Beuret from Rome.[5] Reims Cathedral, whose beauty Rodin's letter describes as "unequaled by anything so far seen in Italy," has the honor of being the first work of Gothic art that he *named*, among his papers now available. It could not have been, however, the first that he *studied*.

Of course there were interruptions, long periods when Rodin had no time for travel, but he has written that whenever he allowed himself a vacation from his studio over a period of forty years and more, he chose faithfully to spend it in the open air, looking for forgotten Gothic and Renaissance works to study and to draw. And year after year he revisited Chartres, Reims, Amiens, and other old friends. His written notes tell us how much he thought of those greatest cathedrals, but his drawings tell us almost nothing of them. For, with the exception of Bourges Cathedral, of which there are three unpublished drawings, Rodin apparently preferred to make his graphic studies of smaller, less famous, monuments, of such churches as Houdan, Montjavoult, and Champeaux. Obviously, he liked to discover neglected works, and, besides that, perhaps the greatest Gothic masterpieces overwhelmed even the great Rodin. At any rate, we know of only one memory sketch of Notre Dame in Paris and one outline of a medallion at Amiens, none of Laon, Le Mans Beauvais, or the others, of which he has written to far the greatest length.

Apparently, since his death, only museum personnel had turned over those loose-leaves of varying sizes on which his travel studies are made, and then, only to add the Musée Rodin stamp and numbers that are written by several hands. Apparently, also, not even the most elementary information had been gathered about these works. Léonce Bénédite approached a first account of them when he wrote his introduction to the second edition of *Les Cathédrales de France*, but he wrote chiefly to justify their exclusion from that small, unillustrated 1921 edition, along with the 109-page introduction to the original 1914 edition.[6] Bénédite, first curator of the Musée Rodin, estimated that there were then in his charge about 800 architectural drawings. Presumably that number included the 100 that came back from the publisher after being reproduced as illustrations for Rodin's book. But the 338 more, now in volume #21594 of the Philadelphia Rodin Museum, could not have been included, for they were not at the Musée Rodin but were bought in 1926 from the collection of Rodin's friend Roger Marx.[7]

We find Bénédite's estimate high if it refers to the number of pages of architectural drawings at the Musée Rodin, but low if it refers to the number of drawings we have seen there, for the drawing pages in Paris have most often more than one sketch recto and verso. Figures 107 and 108, for example, on a page $10\frac{5}{8}$ x $8\frac{7}{10}$ inches, which Rodin folded once, show (*Fig. 107*), two unpublished drawings recto, one on each half page, while verso (*Fig. 108*), Rodin made three sketches on the upper half page and two on the lower half. Thus, seven sketches on a single sheet of paper have only one Musée Rodin number. Many other pages in the Paris Museum Rodin folded twice and then made one drawing in each quarter, so that, in all, the number of drawings is more than double the number of pages.

The pages themselves, the loose-leaves on which Rodin drew, are frequently sheets of printed hotel stationery or else bills for antiques that he bought during his travels. On such paper, the century and the decade are printed in advance, with only the last digit omitted to be filled in by the hotel keeper or merchant. Thus Figure 107 shows that Rodin visited the Hôtel du Saumon at Verneuil and drew there the fifteenth- to sixteenth-century Tour de la Madeleine (*Fig. 109*) during the first decade of the twentieth-century, at any rate before 1910. An-

107. Sheet of unpublished drawings
of the Tour de la Madeleine at Verneuil. Pen and ink over lead pencil.
10⅗ x 8³⁄₁₀ inches. Musée Rodin, Paris
(no. 3349). Photograph by Adelys.

108. Verso of Figure 107.

109. Photographs of the Tour de la
Madeleine at Verneuil.

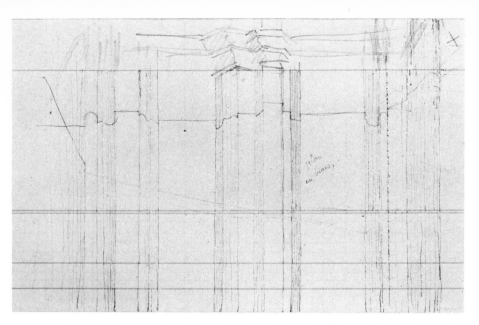

110. Unpublished drawing of architectural forms. Pen and ink over lead pencil. 3 x 4¾ inches. Rodin Museum, Philadelphia Museum of Art. *Actual size.*

111. Unpublished drawing of architectural forms. Ink over pencil. 3 x 4¾ inches. Rodin Museum, Philadelphia Museum of Art. *Actual size.*

112. Drawing of a Renaissance façade, published in Rodin's *Les Cathédrales de France*. Pen and sepia ink. 5⅛ x 3½ inches. Musée Rodin, Paris (no. 5810). Photograph courtesy of Philadelphia Museum of Art. *Actual size.*

113. Unpublished drawing of an imaginary Gothic façade (one of four on a single page). Lead pencil. 3¾ x 3 inches. Musée Rodin, Paris (no. 3607). Photograph by Adelys. *Actual size.*

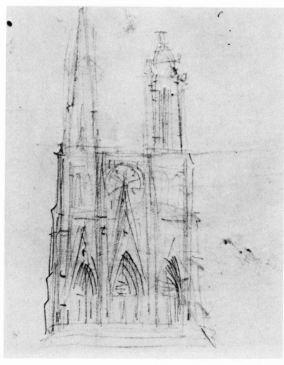

other drawing, Musée Rodin no. 3378, of the south façade of Saint Peter's church at Dreux, is made on another sheet of that same Hôtel Saumon stationery, suggesting that Rodin went from Verneuil to Dreux with a few sheets of Hôtel Saumon paper in his pocket. The earliest complete date to be gathered from all such paper at the Musée Rodin appears on a bill from Le Grand Hôtel de l'Ecu, Sens, Yonne, dated September 24, 1884, on the back of which Rodin has outlined a cornice.

The 338 drawings in Philadelphia, carefully inlaid and bound for their protection, are generally smaller than those in Paris, for they conform to Rodin's pocket-notebook pages, of which the largest measures 5¾₁₆ x 3⅝₁₆ inches and the smallest 3¾₁₆ x 2 inches.[8] Of such little pages, shown here in Figures 110 and 111, a note in Volume 21594 states that they were taken "from five small notebooks filled by Rodin on a tour of France anticipating his book and as the basis of its illustrations."[9]

Bénédite's introduction also announced the presence at the Musée Rodin of a group of Rodin's "original architectural designs." "On trouve," Bénédite wrote, "des dessins originaux d'architecture de rêve." The very idea of architecture imagined by Rodin is intriguing, conjuring up visions of structures to match the fantastic creatures of his imaginative, dark gouache drawings of the 1870's and 1880's. But careful study of the drawings in Paris fulfills no such expectation. Those we believe to be Rodin's "original designs" are more cool and classical than most of his drawings of real architecture. He seems to have prepared us for recognizing them by writing on a few similar designs: "chic," "de mémoire," "petit croquis d'imagination," and "original," none of which are in the folder especially marked: "Dessins d'architecture d'imagination, #3509–3531." Today that folder contains drawings of recognizable, extant chateaux, while the very elegant, evenly divided façades that we take to be Rodin's "dream architectures" are scattered throughout the collection. The majority of these resemble Renaissance dwellings, of which Plate XLVI in Cathédrales (Fig. 112) is typical in that it recalls Rodin's architectural drawings that bear the title "d'àpres Michel Ange." Less frequent are such unpublished sketches as Figure 113, one of four on a page, all suggesting many Gothic façades but exactly like none, and these, after long study, we concluded must be Rodin's fantasies.

Apart from all his imaginative subjects, Rodin's drawing method, often described in connection with his later life-drawings, must always have been the same whether his models were men and women or ancient monuments. Most clearly, simply, and specifically, as it applied to working out of doors, he described that method to Rilke: "j'emploierais la même method que pour mes nus, un rapide contour prie sur le vif que je retoucherais chez moi. Mais avant tout regarder, s'unir, s'identifier à ce qui nous entour" (I would use the same method as for my life drawings, a rapid outline taken from fact that I would go over at home. But first of all observe, be united, identify with what surrounds us).[10]

In such drawings as Figures 107 and 108, we recognize that method as if we were seeing it in action. Clearly, these drawings were set down on the spot, first in pencil and while Rodin's gaze and whole attention were focused on the architecture with which he wished to identify, to be united through understanding. It follows that he would never alter the least detail of such an architecture any more than in his life-drawings he would presume to "correct nature." Simply and precisely, Rodin drew what he saw. And as the architectural drawings piled up, so must his written notes on the same subjects, remaining perhaps as set down until some time between 1900 and 1910. Especially after May 19, 1910, when the contract for *Les Cathédrals* was signed with Armand Colin, Rodin must have chosen from the stack of all his drawings of architecture those that we see in his book.

Many of these book illustrations were not reworked for publication. This we realize now, having seen at the Musée Rodin the actual drawings that the publisher returned. The original drawing for Plate XL in Rodin's book (*Fig. 114*) is on lightweight stationery from the Hôtel de la Coupe d'Or at Houdan and was apparently very swiftly executed, as if in a single stroke. We know that in his later life-drawing Rodin sometimes transferred the outline of a figure to a new page preparatory to a fresh attack on the same subject, which he might already have drawn once or twice. As there are at the Musée Rodin several versions of this same subject, which, by the way, is the flying buttresses and gargoyles of St. Peter's Church at Montfort l'Amaury (*Fig. 115*), we conclude that this particular drawing was made after some practice and with the momentum generated by repetition—not so Rodin's drawing, Plate LXVI in *Cathédrales* (*Fig. 119*). Anyone can see that this handsome drawing was most painstakingly worked over. Yet, despite the trouble and the use of a ruler, there is something wrong with the relative proportions; and also the narrow opening, that is, the entrance, is not in line with the massive arch above. Rodin's drawing of the Episcopal Portal at Sens, (*Fig. 116*), on the other hand, is a perfectly balanced, masterful description of the building (*Fig. 117*). But what the illustration in *Cathédrales*, Plate LXX, does not tell about this drawing is revealed by the paper: that it was made on a page from Rodin's little ledger notebook, ruled in blue horizontally and in red vertically, and that Rodin worked over it so long and hard that there is a hole worn by an eraser right through the middle.[11]

Obviously, the color that Rodin added last to some of these architectural drawings serves a different purpose than the flesh tones of his aquarelles, where it emphasizes the volume and clarifies the arabesque of his figures. The transparent mauve that he spread over some façades and portals expresses the atmosphere in which, by a personal perception,

114. Drawing of buttresses and gargoyles of St. Peter's
Church at Montfort l'Amaury, published in Rodin's *Les
Cathédrales de France*. Pen and ink. 10¾ x 8⅜ inches.
Musée Rodin, Paris (no. 5889). Photograph courtesy of
Philadelphia Museum of Art.

115. Photograph of buttresses and gargoyles of St.
Peter's Church at Montfort l'Amaury.

116. Drawing of the Episcopal Portal at Sens, published in Rodin's *Les Cathédrales de France.* Pen and ink over lead pencil, watercolor wash. 5⅞ x 3¾ inches. Musée Rodin, Paris. Photograph courtesy of Philadelphia Museum of Art.

117. Photograph of the Episcopal Portal at Sens.

118. Photograph of the Portal to St. Peter's Abbey at Auxerre.

119. Drawing of the Portal to St. Peter's Abbey at Auxerre, published in Rodin's *Les Cathédrales de France.* Lead pencil, pen and ink, watercolor wash. 9¾ x 6¼ inches. Musée Rodin, Paris. Photograph courtesy of Philadelphia Museum of Art.

120. Photograph of part of the tympanum of the Portal to St. Peter's Abbey at Auxerre.

121. Drawing detail of the tympanum of the Portal to St. Peter's Abbey at Auxerre, published in Rodin's *Les Cathédrales de France*. Lead pencil, pen and ink, watercolor wash. Size unknown. Musée Rodin, Paris. Photograph courtesy of Philadelphia Museum of Art.

he saw those buildings bathed, and which rather resembles the blue-green spread over his water nymphs to express the tide, while the touches of opaque gray or beige added to certain drawings of buildings express depth.

We might go on taking up one after the other of Rodin's architectural drawings to discover more and more about his resourcefulness; for while throughout all his drawing, his method was constant and true to the description he gave to Rilke, his technical means, called his "facture," were as rich and varied as his appreciation.

The knowledge that Rodin either wholly invented, as in his imaginative works, or drew existing architecture, was for us a promise that he would be a reliable guide to the latter. During many months of following his study trips, of locating and photographing the subjects that he either drew or wrote about, we have been able to verify his reliability. Few of the works he chose to record have altered or disappeared despite wars and restorations, and we were never led astray. Yet to find those works it was highly worthwhile to learn to recognize his taste. For he almost never recorded the name of a church or other building that he drew, and we were lucky where he noted so much as the name of the city or town. This accounts for the numerous illustrations in his book that bear only the title *"étude."*

Everyone knows that in most French cities there are many beautiful historical monuments. At Auxerre, for instance, we looked at a dozen and walked for miles before happening to see, from a distance and on our way back to the station, something that Rodin would at least have *liked,* for we knew by then that he was attracted by the suggestiveness of partly ruined works. So, only by sacrificing our train to our sense of Rodin's taste, we discovered the crumbling sixteenth-century arch of St. Peter's Abbey (*Fig. 118*) the subject of his two drawings Plates LXVI and LXXVI in his book (*Figs. 119 and 121*). And only then, seeing the opening under the arch relatively much wider than in Rodin's drawing, we realized his procedure in that particular work. It was not, of course, that he missed the correct proportions or deliberately altered them, but he had begun his drawing in a smaller size, and then, realizing the interest of the relief in the left of the high tympanum (*Fig. 120*), he simply enlarged the upper portion of his drawing to have room for studying that relief, which he did study separately (*Fig. 121*), leaving the lower part of his drawing as it was, proportionately smaller.

Although by the time Rodin prepared his drawings for publication he no longer remembered where all had been made, any wrong designation, we are convinced, came not from him, who would as soon have used the title *"étude"* for all his illustrations, but came from his editors, who simply guessed. In his book, the church St. Symphorien, for example, is said to be at Chambord, where we looked for it in vain, later finding it at Tours, and still later finding, written on two unpublished drawings, Musée Rodin nos. 3365 and 3368, the notation in Rodin's hand, "St. Symphorien, Tours."

Experiencing Rodin's itinerary, seeking and finding the true subjects of his admiration, however fascinating and however rewarding, is at least equaled by our enjoyment of a group of his architectural drawings that can never be completely identified. These works, whose full identification must always escape us, are, numerous in both the Paris and Philadelphia collections. They have been described as "Rodin's abstractions," first, because he did in fact abstract their subjects from whole architectural works, and, second, because we may appreciate them in the primary way we sometimes appreciate deliberate abstractions, when, for lack of information about the artist's intention, we see and enjoy their execution as much as we are able. This way of seeing these drawings, we believe, is neither contrary nor perverse, for who, being uninformed of their real subjects, can see in such drawings as Figures 110 and 111 more than infinitely sensitive, perfectly controlled, freehand pen-and-ink markings laid on paper? Yet, in the pattern of values formed by the varying weight or lightness of the strokes and in their disposition on the page, which, like music, represents nothing yet suggests many things, there may be keen delight. This unexpected pleasure, unintended by Rodin, is only increased by learning what he *did* intend in these works, even though we cannot follow him all the way. For, of course, we are aware that he never intended to abstract the least element from the architecture that he venerated; on the contrary, he drew fragments only because for him they summarized the whole to which they belonged. It was the marvelous *unity* of those buildings that he admired and, above all, needed. Of the actual subjects of these drawings that we experience as abstractions, Rodin made no mystery. He said they were particular moldings that he strove to render as exactly as possible, moreover labeling them Romanesque, Gothic, or Renaissance.

While no chronological sequence can be now ascribed for these architectural drawings, such very sophisticated shorthand note-taking as that by which all the relative proportions of a building are summarized could only have evolved after years of study.[12] Therefore, we conclude that these "abstractions" must be later than the drawings of whole buildings; and particularly some examples in Philadelphia seem the furthest evolved, although there are superb examples also in Paris. Moreover, on the back of one of his unpublished drawings, Musée Rodin no. 3703, Rodin has written: "*Tout l'ensemble de l'église est retrouvé dans les moulures du sousbasement* (a church in its entirety may be reconstructed from the moldings of it's lower reveals)." This is the thought which, expanded on the last page of his book and followed by forty-four illustrations of moldings alone, seems to say that here, in his drawings of moldings, is the essence and culmination of all Rodin's architectural study.

It is not, however, from these most deliberate and consciously worked of all Rodin's architectural drawings that we best learn how to distinguish between his true life-drawings and their forgeries. It is rather from his drawings made out of doors and left as set down, such as Figures 107 and 108, made without thought of the lines, during a moment of complete immersion in his subject, that we learn Rodin's involuntary stroke. This is his true signature, the native arms that are unavailable to forgers, and particularly in these architectural drawings it comes through most clearly.

While more research remains to be made, from which more connections and conclusions will be drawn, the subjects outlined here may suggest the new perspectives on Rodin and his art that our completed study aspires to open.

The travel, photography and research necessary for this work were made possible by a grant from Chapelbrook Foundation and two grants from the National Endowment for the Humanities. All the photographs of existing architecture were taken by the sculptor Arnold Geissbuhler.—ECG

NOTES

1. This attitude will be considered in my book manuscript now in progress.

2. Paris: Armand Colin, 1914.

3. The English-language edition (Boston: Beacon Press, 1965) reproduces eighty-two drawings or sketches.

4. "Art in Gothic," in *North American Review*, trans. Frederic Lawton (February, 1905), p. 220.

5. Judith Cladel quotes this letter in *Rodin, sa vie glorieuse et inconnue* (Paris: Grasset, Edition Définitive), pp. 110–11.

6. That introduction, almost as long as Rodin's text, was by the Symbolist poet Charles Morice, Rodin's editor. The second, unillustrated edition, published in 1921, was in print to the mid-1950's.

7. We do not know how those notebooks came into the Roger-Marx collection; the name of Clot, the engraver, was mentioned in this connection.

8. Six more drawings in Philadelphia, but not in that volume, are larger.

9. In "Rodin's Abstractions," *Art Journal* (Winter, 1966), that statement is questioned and the paper on which those drawings are made is more fully described and consequently not repeated here.

10. Rilke wrote this statement to his wife, Clara, on the day after he heard it from Rodin—on Wednesday, September 20, 1905. Rilke's letter appeared in *La Revue Bleue* (February, 1938), pp. 100–101.

11. The 1897 reproductions of Rodin's imaginative drawings do give this sort of information by showing all the characteristics of the paper, which in the 1914 edition of *Cathédrales* are completely eliminated.

12. Although the drawings Rodin reworked for his book, and his drawings of whole chateaux, may be equally late, they are a special case and will be treated separately.

True and False*

J. KIRK T. VARNEDOE

In 1962, Ernst Durig died in a hospital in Washington, D.C., leaving among his effects 155 drawings in the manner of Rodin, the large majority signed with Rodin's name. Thought to be authentic—Durig had long claimed to be "Rodin's last pupil"—these drawings were taken over by a prominent auction firm. Prior to their appearance on the market, they were shown to several knowledgeable scholars; almost all of them agreed that the great majority of the drawings were unquestionably forgeries, and they were withheld from sale.

From that point dates consistent study of the problem of forgeries of Rodin drawings. The story of Durig, and the nature of his forgeries,

* The characterizations offered here are based directly on drawings I have studied, and, as much as possible, on works illustrated here; they provide no set formulas that substitute for individual consideration of other drawings attributed to Rodin. A work of art should be judged on its own merits. The admittedly hazardous business of proposing guidelines that extend beyond this stipulation is undertaken only because of the incredible scope of the problem of forgeries of Rodin drawings, and the accompanying injury to proper understanding and appreciation of the artist as a draftsman. I offer the study not as fact but as opinion informed by research whose history I outline below. I am deeply grateful to the owners of the works illustrated here for allowing their drawings to be published in this context.—JKTV

157

was first brought to public attention in the June 4, 1965 issue of *Life* magazine, in an article by Dorothy Sieberling, "The Great Rodin—His Flagrant Faker." The research file compiled for this article establishes beyond doubt Durig's activities as a forger; along with the collection of drawings he left, it is now in The Museum of Modern Art's International Study Center.

In 1967, Rodolfo Paras-Perez, of Harvard University, published "Notes on Rodin's Drawings," *The Art Quarterly* XXX, No. 2 (Summer, 1967), 127 ff. Mr. Perez, after a close reading of Rodin's statements on his own drawings, and after examining not only the Durig collection but also some of the major Rodin collections in the United States proposed several criteria by which authentic and forged drawings could be distinguished.

In early 1969, the Durig collection was sent to Albert Elsen for a final review prior to being declared totally false. With an intensive study of that collection, the present study began.

The Durig collection provided a study resource and touchstone that made Durig's manner subject to both identification and verification. However, no similarly large collection in the United States is indisputably connected with Rodin himself, and thus no certain or verifiable impressions could readily be formed of genuine Rodin draftsmanship. Thus one assumption forced at the outset was that any drawing attributed to Rodin and not in the manner of Durig could be by Rodin. The other initial assumption was that Rodin was a skilled draftsman with a knowledge of the human body; this did not exclude the possibility of a bad authentic drawing, but rather provided a common-sense means of discrimination, a criterion supported by the body of authentic work known.

The first assumption progressively disintegrated; as more and more collections were studied and photographs gathered, many highly dubious drawings began to appear that were clearly not the work of Durig. Over the course of two years' study, these dubious drawings began to fall into distinct groups, separating themselves more and more clearly from each other, from Durig, and especially from Rodin.

The second assumption was progressively reinforced through the study of more and more drawings of indisputable provenance. This included works in major collections in the United States—those of The Art Institute of Chicago, the National Gallery of Art, and The Metropolitan Museum of Art having the most impeccable credentials[1]—and also drawings in European collections. The remarks offered here are based in this experience, and most especially on study in the reserve collection of the Musée Rodin, which is the largest and purest source of original Rodin drawings.[2]

The goal of this latter research was the isolation of those qualities and characteristics unique to authentic Rodin drawings. An attempt to here describe the findings of the study directly, in essay form, would be overly long and finally impractical. Rodin's draftsmanship has proved to be so variegated, in means and technique, that it resists enclosure in definitive statements of what it will always be or, conversely, of what it will never be. Indeed, this very variety is a prime distinguishing factor. Rodin's later drawings have a basis, even if at second hand, in life study, and hence reveal a diversity one would expect from fifteen or more years of changing models and pose experiments; the forgers, on the other hand, tend to be highly consistent, returning again and again to the same format and a characteristic set of conventions and faults.

Taken as a group, Rodin's drawings are difficult to summarize; taken individually, the Rodin forgery is often perplexing. However, by placing the forgery in the company of its fellows and authentic drawings, a pattern becomes evident, and a constellation of attributes emerges by which the forged hand may be recognized. The present study proposes to examine some of the major styles of dubious drawings in this fashion, offering a characterization of those hands that produced enough work to permit individual recognition. By thus enlarging the field of "not Rodin," we reduce the field of authentic Rodin and hopefully gain, in the process, a clearer idea of the latter than would be possible by *a priori* generalizations. This study presumes that the reader is familiar with the points made concerning Rodin's later drawings in the last two sections of the chronological essay in this book.

HAND A

Unfortunately, the only two drawings by this hand available for publication both present back views. Some comments regarding characteristics of frontal views in this style will be made in due course, but a comparison of the two drawings at hand with authentic Rodin works may first point out some of the failings of the forger. In the two Hand A drawings (*Figs. 122 and 123*), the use of repeat lines, the feeling of rapid execution, and the lack of the more refined simplification common to Rodin's Type II watercolors suggest that the Type I drawing was the model imitated, and the forger's selection of paper bears this out. He worked on a wove stock related in general size and characteristics to Rodin's life-drawing paper rather than to the thicker aquarelle paper of Type II.[3]

An initial point of comparison here is the continuity of line movement. The two sides of the back in Figure 123, and particularly the left side, demonstrate the inability of the draftsman to effectuate long line-passages in a single stroke. As previously seen in Figure 59, and as noticeable to a lesser degree in the authentic comparative figures here (*Figs. 124, 125, and 126*), Rodin himself often repeated lines in all or portions of his life-drawings. In an authentic Rodin drawing, however,

122. Formerly attributed to Rodin (here attributed to Hand A): *Standing Nude*, c. 1920. Lead pencil, watercolor wash. 12 x 9¼ inches. Anonymous collection.

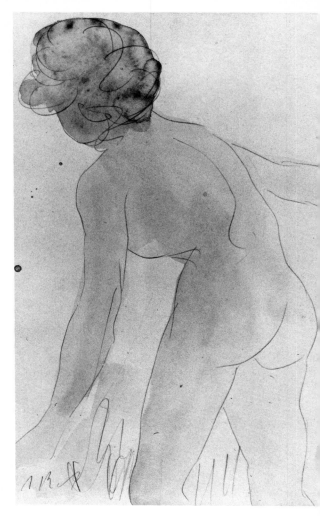

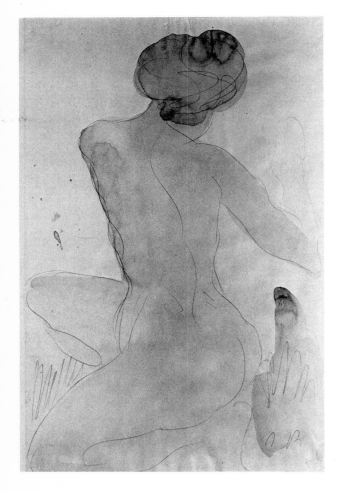

123. Formerly attributed to Rodin (here attributed to Hand A): *Kneeling Nude*, c. 1920. Lead pencil, watercolor wash. 12³⁄₁₆ x 7¹³⁄₁₆ inches. The Art Museum, Princeton University, Princeton, New Jersey.

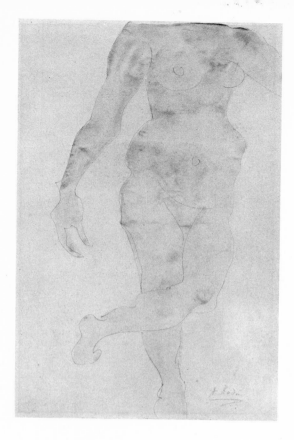

124. *Standing Nude*, c. 1900. Lead pencil, watercolor wash. 11¾ x 7½ inches. Rodin Museum, Philadelphia Museum of Art. Given by Jules Mastbaum.

125. *Kneeling Man*, c. 1905. Lead pencil, watercolor wash. 12¼ x 7¾ inches. Collection, The Museum of Modern Art, New York. Gift of Mr. and Mrs. Patrick Dinehart.

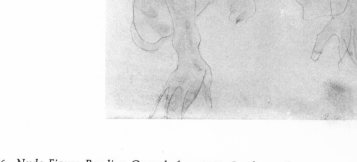

126. *Nude Figure Bending Over*, before 1900. Lead pencil, watercolor wash. 11¾ x 7 inches. Collection of Mr. Martin Revson, New York.

these lines represent multiple essays at the totality, or near-totality, of the portion in question; any one of them, though out of place, conveys information of its own about the form of that section. In the left side of the back of Figure 123, however, the multiple lines are not separate, independently repeated essays, but rather a woven mesh of short strokes used in place of any single attempt to describe the form. There is no one line anywhere in the group that moves from the shoulder to the hip, nor is there among the repeats any significant variation from the normative line sought. This same inability to cover any distance, especially around a curved form, is seen in the treatment of the right knee in Figure 123.

Rodin's line is the bearer of information. By the variety of its movements and the changes of its pressure on the paper, it constantly "reads" the form. If we take any passage of line in the authentic drawings—compare, for example, the left legs of Figures 122 and 124, we will see that the forged line in this style is devoid of any such charge, is bland, and seems only to establish the general location of something in space, providing no information beyond that.

In contrast to the strong sense of bone and flesh structure conveyed by the Rodin drawings, such as Figures 124 and 125, there is no real sense of anatomy in the two inauthentic works. Compare, for example, the left hip in Figure 122 with the hips in Figure 124. Though the latter could hardly be termed an "accurate" depiction of anatomy, it nevertheless conveys a sense of the bone structure beneath the surface, and of the weight being carried by the right leg. The left hip area of Figure 122, on the other hand, is without definition, a rather aimless configuration of four strokes, whose multiple breaks deprive the crucial weight-support point of any strength. The same is true of the hip in Figure 123.

The phenomenon can be seen as well in a comparison of the left hand in Figure 122 with the hands in Figures 124 or 125. In both the authentic drawings, a strong and even exaggerated sense of the differentiation of the wrist from the arm and the hand is established, without break in the line. In the hand areas visible in the two forgeries, by contrast, the line is interrupted just at this point, and the area consequently tends to "float" rather than to carry an analogy of anatomical structure.

Nowhere is the forger's anatomical maladroitness more visible than in the backbone, an area he treated convincingly in only one or two of all his drawings studied. In Figures 122 and 123, the vagaries of an artificially conceived line or lines destroy any sense of the spine as a structural element or of its relation to the body form. The line is based not on observation but on convention.

Hand A employs a consistent format. Virtually all the works are graphite pencil with watercolor wash (no plain pencil drawings have been found).[4] The watercolor of the flesh is of a thin, light tonality, tending toward a yellowish tint. The line is never stomped. The hair wash varies in colors, but it is regularly of the consistency seen in the two illustrations—a watery, uneven solution of pigment that is a fairly effective imitation of Rodin's own wash in such areas.

The Hand A forger was not at all at home with foreshortening and rarely attempted it. He had a preference for back views, and frequently employed other poses with the face averted or partially covered. He also had difficulty in drawing a convincing standing figure, and was strongly disinclined to show a full-length view. Such standing figures as do occur are inevitably severed at the knee or in the lower legs, as in Figure 122, even though the cut-off is far from the edge of the page. Rodin's life-drawings often run off the page; however, as one of the main focuses of Rodin's interest was the fashion in which a figure supports itself, one does not find arbitrary mid-page omissions of support limbs in authentic life-studies.

The figure in this style is almost never shown in any kind of motion beyond that of vague walking, as in Figure 122. There is never an attempt to introduce fantasist elements, such as flying figures, and in fact there are never, beyond occasional drapery, any adjuncts to the single posed figure in the style of Hand A—no couples, no males, no Cambodian dancers, no creatures of mythology, such as the satyress. Nor have any suggestions of reworking been seen.

The general body type has small, high breasts, often in conjunction with a broad back, and hips that swell to a pronounced bulging, though unmuscular thickness across the upper thighs. As has already been suggested, one of the forger's greatest problems lay in drawing convincing joints. He tends to fall down just at the crucial support or pivot points of a figure, usually by breaking his line.

This style has a distinct constellation of formulas for body features. The most common nipple-and-navel conformation is a sidewise V, sometimes with a small loop at the point; an occasional variation of this also appears—an added line which makes the mark a Z sign. The one most consistent variation involves the elimination of the diagonal stroke; seen particularly in the navel, this leaves a configuration of two or three basically horizontal lines, one over the other. The face is built up of these same conventions, the nose base most frequently two parallel lines, the eyes sometimes a Z or V, but most often two curved lines, distinctly separate at the ends, with a single vertical line through the center to suggest the pupil. The forger mistakes his type of drawing in repeating such conventions; in a Rodin life-drawing, such as Figure 125, we see that, in drawing the model rapidly, Rodin did not treat the face conventionally, using instead continuous lines to mark facial form divisions; the type of conventional formula seen in these Hand A drawings resembles instead the faces of the simplified Type II aquarelle, as seen in Figure 130. In these authentic works, the simplifications derive from life notations rather than invariable imagined schemas. If a face is treated summarily in a Rodin life-drawing, it tends to be rendered in a few quick strokes, not with the half-speed care of Hand A. Nipples in Rodin's life-drawing are usually treated in variations of a tight curl, sometimes with a slight angular break at the commencement; the configuration is a taut, springlike one, not slack like those of his imitators.

In the frontal poses of Hand A, the vulval crease is usually rendered in a vertical stroke ending in a vertically elongated loop. In back views, the spinal depression is commonly represented by a hooked stroke (*Fig. 122*). The same hooked curve characterizes the hair; the scramble of these strokes and looping, loose curves, as seen in the heads of both examples illustrated here, is a consistent mark of this style, offering a formless cloud in place of a head shape.

Regardless of pose or size, the other features of format in Hand A are doggedly consistent. There is no heavy, over-all background wash, but there is almost always a splashing of wash outside the figure. This is usually in a pale, neutral tone like that of the flesh, with one or two strokes of a darker wash added in; the wash configurations are usually around the legs of the figure, low on the page, and rarely mount above waist level. What is being imitated here is Rodin's habit, seen in some Type I watercolors, such as Figure 126, of slashing a few trial strokes of wash to one side of the figure.

Very frequently in Hand A drawings the thin lower wash is accompanied by a one- or two-shot spatter trail of denser, darker wash, higher on the page. This trait is perfectly illustrated in Figure 122, but it is also visible in Figure 123. Though this must have been done to give the image verve and a sense of speed in execution, it is often an anomaly, since the splatter is in a watercolor tint not used in the drawing itself.

The lower strokes of thin wash are most often, though not invariably, accompanied by a series of running vertical strokes, clearly visible in both these illustrations, giving the impression that the figure is standing or seated in tall grass. Rodin sometimes made strokes in the ground outside the figure in his Type II aquarelles, but rarely in his life-drawings, except along a contour for reinforcement; gratuitous stroking simply for "heightening" effect is alien to Type I drawings, and the particular kind seen here has only been encountered in Hand A work.

With only one exception, the signature of this hand has always been the same: either at lower right or lower left, an A R of the type seen in the present examples; this is often accompanied by an underlining in the form of a sideways V pointing right. A very similar signature exists on such authentic drawings as Figure 126, however, so this cannot be considered as damning in and of itself. In authentic initial signatures, generally the left upstroke of the A clearly starts from the outside, moving in as it moves up toward the point; the A of the forged signature, by contrast, inevitably begins slightly inside, goes out in a tiny hook and then up to the point. These A's are not crossed but are simply upside-down V's. It should be cautioned that there are undoubtedly many authentic drawings that now bear forged signatures. It is also entirely possible that authentic pencil drawings have been subsequently washed with watercolor by another hand, to increase the market value. Both these alleged practices are well known in the art trade.

Hand A was at work in the last years of Rodin's life, and works by him passed through the hands of at least one prominent collector in the year of the artist's death. This is not really surprising, for these years and the ones immediately following would have been a period in which Rodin's work enjoyed both wide acceptability (this was not true of the drawings of the early years of the century) and high esteem, and the market would have been ripe for exploitation.

Seven drawings in style A were published in *Twelve Aquarelles by Auguste Rodin* (Geneva and Paris, Chez Georg & Cie.) in 1920. Hand A works were sold on the Paris market in the 1920's, but the drawings have not been seen in trade in recent years. A selection of drawings in this mode was used to illustrate at least one 1960's publication on Rodin; they came from a French collection, but drawings in the style are found in the United States as well.

HAND B

In the case of Hand B, we are fortunate in having a broader range of illustrations; as these tend to speak for themselves, explanation need not be as extensive. This style does not attempt to imitate the rapid, repeat-stroked sketches of Rodin but aspires to the refined simplicity of the second-stage watercolors, exemplified by the authentic works in Figures 128, 130, and 133. As did Hand A, this imitator chose his paper according to the type of authentic work he copied. He was even more diligent, in fact, frequently working on a thick marked watercolor paper that Rodin himself used from time to time.[5] He tended also to a large format: 18 to 20 inches in height by 11¾ to 13 inches in width are the common measurements, though smaller works such as Figures 129 and 131 are not exceptionally rare.

One of the most evident attributes of the style is a recurrent body type (*Figs. 127, 129, and 134*). Figure 127 provides an extreme demonstration: small, flat breasts on a short, rather flabby torso, with broad hips atop a disturbingly long lower body, with thick knees and thighs. Though the type seems individual in each case at first view, exposure to several drawings by the same hand reveals, even when facial arrangement, hair, and some proportional areas are changed, a constant return to this basic formula. The three Rodin nudes shown here (*Figs. 128, 130, and 133*), on the other hand, have distinctly individual, varied figure forms.

In an authentic Type II drawing (*Figs. 128 and 130*), the form of the

127. Formerly attributed to Rodin (here attributed to Hand B): *Standing Nude*, c. 1917–20. Lead pencil, watercolor wash. 20 x 12¾ inches. Anonymous collection.

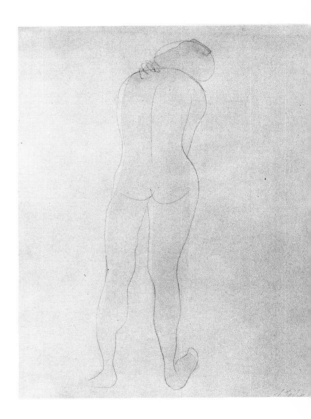

128. *Standing Nude*, c. 1905. Lead pencil, watercolor wash. 12¼ x 9⅛ inches. Rodin Museum, Philadelphia Museum of Art. Given by Jules Mastbaum.

129. Formerly attributed to Rodin (here attributed to Hand B): *Standing Nude*, c. 1917. Lead pencil, watercolor wash. 12⁵⁄₁₆ x 9¼ inches. Worcester Art Museum, Worcester, Massachusetts.

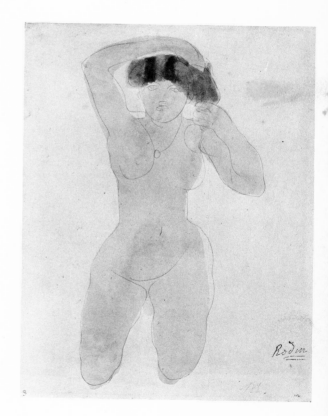

130. *Kneeling Nude*, c. 1900. Lead pencil, watercolor wash. 12¾ x 9⅞ inches. Courtesy of The Art Institute of Chicago.

131. Formerly attributed to Rodin (here attributed to Hand B): *Cambodian Dancer*, c. 1917–20. Lead pencil, watercolor wash. 12¼ x 9⅜ inches. Anonymous collection.

132. *Cambodian Dancer*, 1906. Lead pencil, watercolor wash. 12¼ x 9⅜ inches. Collection of Mrs. Jefferson Dickson, Beverly Hills.

133. *Two Figures*, c. 1905. Lead
pencil, watercolor wash. 12⅞ x
9¹³⁄₁₆ inches. National Gallery
of Art, Washington, D.C. Gift
of Mrs. John W. Simpson.

134. Formerly attributed to Rodin (here attributed to Hand B): *Two Figures*, c.
1917–20. Lead pencil, watercolor wash. 11½ x 13¼ inches. The Baltimore Museum
of Art.

135. Formerly attributed to Rodin (here attributed to Hand B): *Kneeling Figure*, c. 1917. Lead pencil, watercolor wash. 12⅜ x 9¼ inches. Worcester Art Museum, Worcester, Massachusetts.

body is highly abstracted, and detailing of internal features is reduced to a minimum. Though the steady unbroken contour of style B attempts to imitate the handling of a drawing like Figure 128, the forger bastardized the style by including a certain stock set of details—for instance, in the stomach area of Figures 127 and 129, flesh folds and a superfluous rib-cage line, respectively. The knee-cap convention, seen as it is in these drawings or in slight modifications, is common to this hand. It conveys nothing about what is occurring anatomically. Rodin included such details when they informed—as in the right, weight-bearing leg of the standing woman in Figure 133. When he did, the detail was derived from observation rather than stock formula. Forger B, by contrast, maintained the conventions used for nipples in Figures 127 and 129—a roughly circular broad oval, half-moon or more fully closed—without consideration for changes in form effected by changes in position or point of view. The attention to some details does not, then, produce any greater anatomical accuracy; the carefully lined six toes on the left foot of Figure 127 affirm this. The added lines contribute nothing in return for what they destroy; the drawing never arrives at the simplicity of a Type II aquarelle and remains a more standard life-drawing (albeit undoubtedly not done from life) of an unconvincing and uninteresting nature.

The forger's hesitancy between simplicity and detail is rooted in

136. Formerly attributed to Rodin (here attributed to Hand B): Signature. Anonymous collection.

inability as well as misunderstanding; he was incapable of the decisive sweep of line that characterizes a Rodin drawing such as Figure 130. Though the style B lines move in and out in an attempt to suggest a concern with form (see the hips of Figure 129) it stays within a lumpy columnar body silhouette, with no sense of the stresses within the body; compare, for example, the treatment of the groin and abdominal areas in Figure 129 and Figure 130. When the body is reduced to a contour, the frequency of that line's movement, its density, its speed, become the bases on which the drawing lives or dies. In style B, it dies a plodding, deliberate death. The single most distinguishing, and damning, feature of this hand is the heavy-handed, wooden line seen in Figure 135. As it tracks slowly up and around contours, cautiously moving in or out occasionally, the line almost never varies from its hesitant pace or medium-pressure density. This imparts to the finished whole a stiff, brittle quality that is the antithesis of the focused energy of the Rodin contour.

Nowhere is this stiffness more evident than in the forger's attempt at Cambodian dancers, of which we have an example in Figure 131. In the authentic Rodin dancer (*Fig. 132*), there is a sense of the effective continuity of the body through the arms and across the shoulders, up from the legs to the head. In Figure 131, however, the arms, head, and feet appear to be cut-out appendages pasted down beside the shape of the costume. In place of the rapid, bold stroke movements of the authentic dancer, we have a tight, niggling concern with the rendering of the hat and shoulder protrusions of the costume. The forger has sought to imitate Rodin's simplification of the feet, but has been indecisive; maintaining the general enlongated shape, he abandoned the quick line, and, in keeping with his misunderstanding, noted the two ankle bones. A comparison of the faces in two authentic Rodin drawings (*Figs. 130 and 132*), with those in two style B drawings (*Figs. 129 and 131*), shows that the forger shied from the rapidity of life execution and the abstraction of the second-stage watercolor. His attempts at foreshortening (note the face in Figure 129) look clumsy beside the easy expertise of Rodin (*Fig. 133*).

In an attempt to enliven the stick-figure rigidity of the Cambodian dancer, forger B dashed a few meaningless lines about the background, as he did not uncommonly in many other drawings.

Hand B, unlike Hand A, ventured into more complicated formats (*Fig. 134*). Several lesbian couples in this mode have been seen, and the forger often used full background washes similar to the one at hand; the kind of elaborate two-tone "landscape" setting evoked by the wash here is unlike the wash handling of Rodin, who probably would not have taken the same care in brushing around the hand and foot at the right of Figure 134. The wash in the lower right part of this drawing displays a technique sometimes seen in authentic works but much favored by

Hand B: a mottled application of mixed wash, resulting in "explosion" patterns of color. In such cases, and in the dresses of his Cambodian dancers, Hand B tends to prefer mixes of strong hues, achieving phosphorescent effects in yellows, greens, oranges, and blues.

Figure 129 is rather unusual, as, in contrast to Hand A, this imitator more frequently avoids cutting the body, preferring to treat the full-length form. Two or three difficult poses have been seen in this mode, usually in reclining figures, but most often the attitudes selected are stable, consciously struck poses. In one case, Hand B introduced a note of fantasy into one of his large, heavily washed aquarelles, in the form of a satyr struggling with a woman. Such conceptions can be identified by their misunderstanding of the role of fantasy in Rodin's later drawings. In a gouached drawing of the late 1870's or the 1880's, a satyr would have been conceived and set down as such; however, in the life-based drawings of the post-1896 period, mythological creatures are formed by the reworking or adjustment of life-drawings, and their origin is recognizable. Furthermore, scenes of struggle, such as those of the "black" drawings, do not occur in the large watercolors of Rodin's later years, which are characterized by a more voyeurist sexuality.

The signature of Hand B varies from "Aug Rodin" to "A Rodin," in a handwriting whose deadened evenness of pencil pressure is similar to that remarked in the drawing contours (*Fig. 136*). The "d" is also consistent in its basic configuration, in that the stroke leading from the loop to the "i" is usually horizontal, regardless of its point of departure.

With steady consistency, works in this style have been found to trace back to a single common provenance: the collection of a lady who knew Rodin quite well after 1900, and who wrote a couple of small articles on him prior to 1910. This collection also included some authentic drawings—one dedicated to her in Rodin's hand—and how the large number of forgeries came into the lady's possession is unknown. She sold large numbers of them soon after Rodin's death, including a bulk of more than 100 sheets to a prominent New York firm (from whence comes the Worcester Art Museum collection, which includes Figures 129 and 135, acquired in 1918). A final part of the collection, including two authentic sheets, appeared on the market in 1969 but was declined by the major London auction houses. Drawings in this mode have been published in works on Rodin and are found in museum collections in the United States, Britain, France, the Orient, and elsewhere.

ERNST DURIG

Ernst Durig poses, at the outset, fewer problems than either Hand A or Hand B, in that he is the only forger for whom we have not only a name, but also a large source collection directly attributable.

137. Formerly attributed to Rodin (here attributed to Ernst Durig): *Nude Figure*, c. 1930. Lead pencil, watercolor wash. 12⅞ x 10 inches. Anonymous collection.

138. *Nude Figure*, c. 1902–6. Lead pencil, watercolor wash. 9¾ x 12¾ inches. Princeton University Library, Princeton, New Jersey.

139. *Nude Figure*, c. 1905. Lead pencil. 9¾ x 12³⁄₁₆ inches. Courtauld Institute of Art, London. Witt Collection.

140. Formerly attributed to Rodin (here attributed to Ernst Durig): *Two Figures*, c. 1930. Lead pencil, watercolor wash. 22 x 16¼ inches. Anonymous collection.

141. *Two Figures*, c. 1905. Lead pencil, watercolor wash, gouache. 12¾₁₆ x 9⅞ inches. The Metropolitan Museum of Art, New York. Kennedy Fund, 1910.

However, the diversity in certain aspects of Durig's work makes it the most difficult to characterize. There is an enormous variation in quality within the production, and, though in this aspect the work almost never approaches Rodin's own drawings closely enough to cause serious doubt, it makes broad statements of his deficiencies less easy. Furthermore, Durig did not enclose himself within any set formula of materials or format. Though he most often worked in soft graphite pencil and watercolor, as seen in Figure 140, he also did plain pencil drawings, ink drawings (*Fig. 142*), charcoals (*Fig. 145*), and even a series of etchings.[6] He worked very frequently on a large, thick aquarelle paper (not of the quality of that used by Rodin), but also produced drawings on a small, finer wove paper.[7] Nor did he select any one strain of Rodin drawings to imitate. He produced drawings based on the gouached manner of the 1880's, on the Cambodian dancers, and on the pen sketches Rodin used for small notations and explanatory figures,[8] as well as on standard aquarelles of the nude. He did not depend on a consistent type of invented pose but attempted a wide range, often copying his poses directly from those in published Rodin drawings,[9] and did not shy from attempting the unusual and difficult attitudes favored by Rodin.

Figure 137 shows that Durig was willing, as other forgers were not, to go beyond an image of ordinary "prettiness" to one of sensationalism or even grotesqueness. In this sense, he was closer to Rodin, as the artist himself did not preoccupy himself with the appeal of his drawings. Rodin frequently produced images that were visually unappealing in any marketable sense; and by his choice of poses, his images often went beyond the bland, if mildly titillating, propriety that characterizes most of the forgeries.[10]

However Figure 137 is only an imitation of a pose type, failing to approach either the quality or the intention of similar Rodin works (*Figs. 138 and 139*). Figure 138 shows Rodin's more detached concern with the synthesis, the reduction to essentials, of a difficult view of the human form; Figure 139 shows the uncompromising specificity of his curiosity concerning every aspect of the body. The Durig drawing, while attempting to exploit salable sensationalism, has no such clear goals in mind. Compared to the two Rodin works, both its handling and posture seem bland and noncommittal. Durig's use of stomping should be noted here; he smudges the pencil to indicate volume (in the breasts) and to create coloristic effects (in the pubic hair). Rodin would never give so much attention to the purely coloristic area, as his interest was primarily in form; indeed, he usually did not include any suggestion of pubic hair at all in his watercolors. Furthermore, it would be unlike Rodin to define the two small breast volumes so strongly while leaving the major forms totally unmodeled. Perhaps Durig hoped by such stresses to draw attention from some basic deficiencies, such as the ambiguity of the right arm below the elbow, or the connection of the waist and shoulders on the figure's right side.

Figure 140 is typical of the large format drawings beloved of Durig, and is symptomatic as well of some of his major failings. He gives us a male-female couple, a combination not yet seen in an authentic late drawing; the embraces in Rodin's late production are, as in Figure 141, uniquely lesbian. In spite of several corrections in the legs on the left of Figure 141, we have no difficulty in understanding how each figure is placed in space, or how it supports itself. The Durig couple projects no such certainty, particularly in regard to the woman at the left, who is either kneeling, falling, or simply floating in space. We might further wonder about the relation in size between the two Durig figures, if we envision the woman standing full-length beside this man, whose upper left arm, from shoulder to elbow, appears to be one-third longer than his torso.

The "floating" figure is a common deficiency in Durig's work; not only did he have trouble in describing convincingly the effects of gravity on normal figures, but he also favored occasional flying poses (*Fig. 142*). Rodin himself played with gravity in his later drawings, but in the following way: Having done a drawing from the model, he would take the pose, or a tracing of it, and change the orientation of the page by jotting the word "*bas*" (bottom) on the side he preferred as base. In this way he obtained a spatially freed figure, and, in at least two cases known, he added figures or landscape below to suggest that the figure was indeed flying. He liked the suggestions afforded by such new points of view, and would sometimes also note a title relating to a natural form, such as a tree, which the body suggested in its new orientation. In such authentic works, it is possible to determine the original position of the figure; the artist's reckoning with the support of the body in the life-drawing will remain. In Durig's work, the figure is imagined as weightless from the outset, and the drawing will not work as a life rendering regardless of directional considerations.

The same problem besets some of Durig's imaginary couples. Not only in the cut-outs, but also in combination tracings (*Fig. 90*), Rodin sometimes brought together figures of separate orientation and scale into a new ensemble; in such a case, however, the figures remain individually viable, regardless of the fantasy of their new juxtaposition. This type of ensemble, obviously the product of some tracing or transfer, is found virtually exclusively in the Type II watercolor format. Durig, however, conceives groups like those in Figure 142, as well as more elaborate three-woman ensembles (yet to be seen in an authentic late drawing), one behind the other, or interlocked, soaring across the page in a style imitative of the rapid repeat-stroking of a life-drawing.

These latter images are in line with a visionary and Utopian strain in Durig's work. He not only forged Rodin sculptures but did statues of his own, including a *Monument to Peace* and a work called *The World of Tomorrow*, which was a hybrid of Rodin's *Springtime* and *Love Turning the World* in format. His admiration for Mussolini no doubt derived

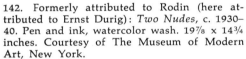

142. Formerly attributed to Rodin (here attributed to Ernst Durig): *Two Nudes*, c. 1930–40. Pen and ink, watercolor wash. 19⅞ x 14¾ inches. Courtesy of The Museum of Modern Art, New York.

143. Formerly attributed to Rodin (here attributed to Ernst Durig): *Cambodian Dancer*, c. 1930–40. Lead pencil, watercolor wash. 13½ x 11 inches. The Baltimore Museum of Art.

144. *Cambodian Dancer*, 1906. Lead pencil, water-color wash. 12¾⁄₁₆ x 9¼ inches. The Maryhill Museum of Art, Maryhill, Washington.

145. Formerly attributed to Rodin (here attributed to Ernst Durig): *Mother and Child*, c. 1940–55. Charcoal. The Museum of Modern Art International Study Center, New York. Durig Collection.

146. *Mother and Children*, c. 1880.
Pen and ink, gouache. 7⅛ x 5⅛
inches. Rodin Museum, Philadelphia
Museum of Art. Given by Jules Mastbaum.

147. Formerly attributed to Rodin (here
attributed to Ernst Durig): Signature.
The Museum of Modern Art International Study Center, New York. Durig
Collection.

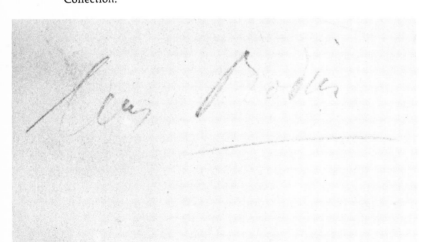

148. Imitation of the collector's mark of
Odilon Roche (Lugt, 2007e). 4 x 5 mm
(⅙ x ⅕ inches).

from similar currents in his alternately tragic and comic psyche. In his drawings, this strain comes to light not only in his "golden age" visions of nude male and female couples, and in his imitations of the powerful mother figures of Rodin's "black" drawings (*Fig. 145*); (he was the only major forger to attempt this style), but also in a generally very large, muscular female type, with broad shoulders and relatively thick joints. It also no doubt figures in his preference for theatrical expressions of exaggerated melancholy or ecstasy on the faces of many of his nudes.

In his grasp of anatomy, Durig varied from the nearly successful to the comically impossible. He, like Hand B, sketched a six-toed foot at times (*Fig. 140*) and also had considerable trouble with joints, which tend to be either out of place or practically nonexistent. Rodolfo Paras-Perez suggested an explanation for this, pointing out that Durig frequently put the flesh wash on the page first and then was obliged to adjust his anatomical lines to fit it. Paras-Perez also suggested that, since Rodin's watercolors always proceeded from a base drawing, which was then washed, the sequence of materials on the page is one method of distinguishing a forgery; this is a valuable idea but has proved less effective than might be hoped in actual practice.[11]

Durig's work does not seem to be susceptible, because of the variety of his production, to recognition by a specific set of shorthand formulas. He does tend toward two types of nipples: one, when the breast is in profile, is a separate small circle, sometimes joined to the major contour line by an added covering line. In frontal views, his nipples and navels are often indicated in a very loose, quick, single loop, with the crossing ends of the lines extended; these loops lack the tautness of their counterparts in authentic drawings.

Unlike Hand A or Hand B, Durig varies his line weight markedly. In fact, his signature (*Fig. 147*) is often recognizable in terms of its distinct rhythm of widely different thick and thin strokes. Moreover, Durig often covered a broad area in a rapid stroke. He maintained the same basic style of line work—fast and loose, with some *pentimenti* regardless of format. The variety and rapidity of Durig's line is not informed by close observation, as the Cambodian dancer in Figure 143 demonstrates. The image lacks the continuity of a Rodin life-drawing, as we are left in doubt as to what happens to the waist. There is a further ambiguity, too, about structure and proportional relationships in the area from the waist to the knees. As Figure 144 shows, Rodin's drawings are not flawless in this regard either; a discrepancy in the arm lengths is noticeable. However, the structure of the body in the Rodin dancer is sound and legible, and no part of the drawing taxes the credibility to the extent of the rubbery right arm of Durig's figure.

Another mistake Durig made with his Cambodian dancers from time to time was to show them topless. No contemporary reports of their visit to France nor any scholarship on Cambodian dances suggests that this could have been the case when Rodin drew them; it would have been particularly unlikely at the public practice session at which he seems to have done most of the drawings. Furthermore, photographs clearly show that the tiny dancing girls, even were they ever topless, would not have displayed the physical endowments suggested by Durig's images of them.[12]

The pointed drop of watercolor in the area of the Durig dancer's left ear is a trademark of Durig's wash treatment and often appears on a larger scale. Durig preferred a relatively even (though often a too pink or too yellow) flesh wash, and set it off frequently by dark hair and background washes, preferring a brown for the hair. His wash almost never shows the type of irregular pigment solution of Rodin's own watercolors, but is denser, more even, and leaves a more regular tint.

The deficiencies of Durig's imitation of the gouached style (*Fig. 145*) seem so obvious in the comparison at hand (*Fig. 146*) as to need little discussion; in place of the mixed spontaneity of pen and thick solidity of gouache development in the Rodin, Durig gives us a series of sausage-like forms, with none of the complications of facture found in a Rodin "black" work.

Durig was a latecomer. He apparently did not begin as a forger until he came to the United States in 1928, and the major period of his activity came in the 1930's and 1940's. He forged Pascin and Maillol as well, but Rodin was his obsession. It was a matter that went beyond monetary objectives, for Durig produced his incredibly large forged *oeuvre* in a period when prices on the Rodin market were depressed, and he apparently profited little from his efforts. Durig drawings tend to be found in large groups—one private collection of more than 250 sheets has been seen—and they appear frequently on the New York art market, despite the continuing efforts of scholars and concerned dealers to impede this trade. A good deal of Durig's work found its way into collections in the Los Angeles area, and, in the 1940's, a San Francisco department store sold a group of Durigs as the purported collection of a war refugee. His work has frequently been published as authentic Rodin, and it is found in a great many museum and private collections in all parts of the United States.

PSEUDO-ROCHE

One other major hand should be mentioned, even though, unfortunately, we have no photograph to publish as an illustration. The style is connected with one prime distinguishing feature: a collector's mark purporting to be that of Odilon Roche.

In his *Marques des Collections des Dessins et des Estampes* (*Supplément*), of 1956, Fritz Lugt gives a brief biographical sketch of Odilon Roche, a rather important figure in the history of Rodin drawings. Roche was connected with the commercial transactions of the Musée Rodin in the 1920's. He built a large collection of Rodin drawings, and, subsequently, his collector's mark became recognized as a good provenance for a Rodin drawing.

It has been a common practice on the art market to mark a mediocre but authentic work with an imitation of a well-respected collector's mark in order to increase its value. In some cases, the forged Roche *cachet* may have been so applied. However, in the course of the present study, it has become evident that this forged mark is connected, with a very high degree of frequency, with drawings of dubious authenticity; Lugt mentions in his article on the mark that the false *cachet* appears frequently on forgeries.

The style of drawing associated with this fake *cachet* is not so unvarying as to lend itself to easy characterization. All of the ones so far studied appear to be in imitation of Type III aquarelles; that is, they show no body distortions, do not favor strongly energetic poses, will have some *pentimenti*, and frequently favor a stomped background or muted-color wash heightening. A secondary strain, apparently by the same hand, tends to a sparser image, with practically no *pentimenti* and no background elaboration. In this latter style, which curiously enough does not always appear with the *cachet*, a particular anatomical misunderstanding recurs; in foreshortened poses, the portions receding into space become larger than the foreground elements.

Without available illustrations, it would be futile to pursue a style as clever and diffuse as this. Furthermore, not all drawings seen by this hand carry the forged mark, and all the drawings bearing the mark do not fall easily into practical definitions. Certainly the false *cachet* should not be considered damning in and of itself. However, the *amateur* and student of Rodin's work should be well aware of it, and for that reason we publish it here (*Fig. 148*). By comparing this mark to the authentic Roche mark reproduced in Lugt's book (no. 2007e, p. 292), one can see that the forgery misunderstands the relationship between the letters and the surrounding box. A London dealer passed along a helpful rule of thumb to me in this regard: in the original *cachet*, it would be possible to place an O of the same size both above and below the O in the mark, without exceeding the limits of the box. This would be impossible in the forged *cachet*, for the letters are too large. Lugt mentions another forgery of the *cachet*, in which the periods following the letters are not the same; though I have never seen this second imitation, I have been told by a knowledgeable dealer in Paris that it errs by omitting the period following the R.

The forged *cachet* appears to date back into the early 1930's, but drawings bearing its impress have been turning up with great frequency in recent years. Of all Rodin drawings, the Type III aquarelle is the most susceptible to imitation. Authentic drawings of this type appear far less frequently on the market than any other type of late Rodin drawing, yet forged imitations appear regularly.

NOTES

1. The large collection of drawings in the Rodin Museum in Philadelphia has a good reputation of long standing, but it cannot be considered as beyond question, as the collection was purchased through a Parisian dealer in the 1920's, rather than directly from the Musée Rodin in Paris. The Art Institute of Chicago and The Metropolitan Museum of Art each have several drawings either bought from or given by Edward Steichen or Alfred Stieglitz, both of whom (especially Steichen) were closely involved with Rodin's drawings during the artist's lifetime. Many of the Metropolitan's drawings were purchased in 1910, out of the exhibition at the "291" Gallery. The drawings in the National Gallery's collection were given by Mrs. John W. Simpson, who knew Rodin well; most of the Simpson drawings and prints bear a dedication from the artist.

2. The collection of the Musée Rodin cannot, unfortunately, be considered to be above all question. First, the situation in Rodin's studio, particularly in the confused last years of his life, makes it possible that other drawings may have found their way into the collection. Secondly, the Musée has not only received drawings as donations in the past but has purchased drawings at auction; since no system of cataloguing keeps these later additions distinct from the base collection formed at the time of Rodin's death, adulteration of the collection is not at all unlikely.

3. There is no consistency of sheet size in these drawings. Among those studied, the most common size was about 12¼ inches in height by about 7¾ to 9 inches in width, with a secondary variant in the range of about 11½ by about 7½ inches. The papers examined were about four-thousandths of an inch thick, with a regular mechanical texture seen by transmitted light. A fine mechanical toothing was clearly visible on the smooth surface of all sheets.

4. There are some sheets in pen and watercolor corresponding closely in wash characteristics, signature, and so on, to this manner. These variants show poses that can be traced to Rodin drawings reproduced in the artist's lifetime and seem to be the result of copying, if not tracing, from the line reproductions. The figures on these sheets are generally a good deal smaller than the usual Hand A works, and a great deal smaller than the Rodin works they imitate. Regrettably, almost all such variants seen have been studied in photograph only, and I can provide no further information about them.

5. Hand B often worked on a paper that bears all or part of the following impressed mark: B CRAYON * ANC^ne MANUF^re * CANSON & MONTGOLFIER * VIDALON-LES-ANNONAY. Rodin himself used this paper from time to time; it is found, for example, in some of the Cambodian-dancer drawings. Hand B also used a thick watercolor paper with a very heavily toothed surface.

6. Rodin's own drypoint prints can be easily checked by referring to Loys Delteil, *Le Peintre-Graveur Illustre*, VI (1910) (see also additional plates mentioned in note 89 in my earlier chapter). The etchings made by Durig are eleven plates, printed in brown ink, including: two Cambodian dancers, one topless; three nude dancing figures with long transparent draperies, one group of three standing nudes; and five scenes of nude females with children. The latter five scenes showed a confusion of earlier imaginative motifs and later aquarelle mode, including not only the children, but symbolic globes, in imaginary visions of flying ensembles.

7. Durig's large aquarelle paper is frequently seen with a "chalky-eggshell finish which masks the fibers," as Paras-Perez pointed out in "Notes on Rodin's Drawings." It apparently came in tablet form, as Durig sheets are frequently found with a wide band of gummed paper attached to the top edge.

8. The pen style Durig imitated is that used by Rodin in the drawings reproduced in *Briefe an Zwei Deutschen Frauen*, a compilation of letters from Rodin put together by Helene von Nostitz. Among the drawings Durig did in this manner were a series purporting to represent the Russian ballet dancer Nijinsky; many of these are now in the collection at The Museum of Modern Art's International Study Center.

9. Durig copied a wide variety of Rodin poses, imitating not only published later drawings but drypoints and sculpture as well. The collection at The Museum of Modern Art International Study Center contains a number of drawings whose poses derive directly from those in the folio edition of reproductions, *Rodin* (Paris: Galerie d'Estampe, 1933), with an introduction by Georges Grappe.

10. Forgers may have shied from imitating Rodin's so-called pornographic drawings because such works might be more difficult to sell. I have seen in photograph one forgery, not by any of the hands described here, which showed cunnilingus between two lesbians. Nothing of this type has yet been seen among authentic drawings, though lesbian embraces are common.

11. As Paras-Perez pointed out in "Notes on Rodin's Drawings," Rodin watercolors frequently show many levels of work, with pencil stroking both over and under wash passages. He is certainly correct in stating, though, that the basic body-lines of a Rodin watercolor drawing should always lie under the wash; he is also correct in pointing out that, in the case of Durig, the pencil is found frequently to be *over* the wash. However, as a practical criteria for distinguishing forgeries, this has limitations. First of all, not all forgers made the Durig mistake, and even Durig was not totally consistent in this regard. Furthermore, it is often extremely difficult to judge the wash-and-pencil sequence of a drawing with anything short of microscopic inspection. This is particularly true with regard to watercolors faded by sunlight.

12. There are some topless Cambodian dancers among authentic Rodin drawings; they are males. Research by John Tancock, Curator of the Rodin Museum, Philadelphia, produced the affirmation from Cambodian information services that the dancers never appeared topless or nude. For further reference to the Cambodians and Rodin's connection with them, see the section on the Cambodians and Note 139 in my earlier chapter.

Chronological Guide

1854–60	Student years at the Petite Ecole. Independent drawing study.	*Figures* 2, 3, 4, 5, 6, 19(?)
1860–64	Early work as apprentice sculptor. Continued study, course with Barye.	*Figures,* 7, 8, 9, 10, 11, 12, 13
1864–75	Work in studio of Carrier-Belleuse. To Brussels, 1870. Independent study and sculptural work.	*Figures* 14, 15, 17
1875–76	Trip to Italy, influence of Michelangelo.	*Figures* 21, 22, 23, 24, 25, 26
1877–78	Return to Paris. *The Age of Bronze.*	*Figures* 20, 31, 32, 33, 34
1879–80	Work at Sèvres. *St. John the Baptist.*	*Figures* 27, 28, 29, 36
Late 1870's–early 1880's *(see also 1864–75 discussion in text)*	Gouache manner.	COLOR PLATE I; *Figures* 16, 18, 65, 91, 104, 105

1880–82	Early work on *The Gates of Hell.* First drypoint prints.	*Figures* 38, 39, 40, 41, 42, 43
1883	Drypoint prints. Life studies of Victor Hugo.	*Figures* 35, 44, 45, 46, 49
1884–85	Drypoint prints. *Enguerrande* illustrations.	*Figures* 47, 50, 55, 56
1885–90	Reduction in graphic work(?). Baudelaire illustrations, 1887–88.	*Figures* 51, 52, 53, 54, 57, 58
1890–93	Frontispiece for *La Vie Artistique.* Portraits.	*Figures* 63, 64, 70, 72; *Frontispiece*
1894–96	Inception of late drawing manner(?).	*Figures* 66, 67, 69
1897–1900	Emergence of late drawing manner. Publications of late drawings. Exhibitions. Termination and exhibition of *Balzac.*	*Figures* 59, 60, 61, 62, 68, 73, 75, 78, 90, 126
1900–1905	Further development of late manner. *Découpages.*	Color Plates III, IV; *Figures* 74, 76, 79, 80, 84, 89, 92, 93, 94, 95, 96, 97, 99, 100, 101, 102, 141
1906	*Cambodian Dancers.*	Color Plate II; *Figures* 87, 88, 132, 144
1907–8	Establishment of studio at Hôtel Biron. Large exhibitions of drawings.	*Figures* 77, 85, 86
1908–15	Increased use of stomping in pencil work. Abandonment of watercolor wash(?).	*Figure* 82

Selected Bibliography

BOOKS ON RODIN

Bénédite, Léonce. *Rodin.* Paris: F. Rieder & Cie, 1926.

Bourdelle, Emile-Antoine. *La Sculpture et Rodin.* Paris: Emile-Paul, 1937.

Cladel, Judith. *Auguste Rodin pris sur la vie.* Paris: Editions de La Plume, 1903.

―――. *Auguste Rodin, l'oeuvre et l'homme.* Brussels: Van Oest, 1908.

―――. *Rodin, sa vie glorieuse et inconnue.* Paris: Grasset, 1950 (Definitive Edition).

Coquiot, Gustave. *Le Vrai Rodin.* Paris: J. Tallandier, 1913.

―――. *Rodin à l'hôtel de Biron et à Meudon.* Paris: Oliendorf, 1917.

Delteil, Loys. *Rude, Barye, Carpeaux, Rodin—Le Peintre-graveur illustré XIX et XX siecles, Vol. VI.* Paris: Delteil, 1910.

Descharnes, Robert, and Chabrun, Francois. *Rodin.* New York: Viking Press, 1967.

Elsen, Albert (ed.). *Auguste Rodin, Readings on His Life and Work.* (contains "Auguste Rodin, Sculptor," by Truman Bartlett; "Auguste Rodin," by Rainer Maria Rilke; and "Rodin's Reflections on Art," by Charles-Etienne Henri Dujardin-Beaumetz). Englewood Cliffs, N.J.: Prentice Hall, 1965.

*―――. *Rodin.* New York: The Museum of Modern Art, 1963.

―――. *Rodin's Gates of Hell.* Minneapolis: University of Minnesota Press, 1960.

Gantner, Joseph. *Rodin und Michelangelo.* Vienna: Schroll, 1953.

†Geissbuhler, Elisabeth C. *Rodin—Later Drawings.* Boston: Beacon Press, 1963.

Goldscheider, Cécile, and Jianou, Ionel. *Rodin.* Paris: Arted, 1967.

Grappe, Georges. *Catalogue du Musée Rodin.* Paris: Editions of 1929, 1931, 1934, 1938, 1944.

Lawton, Frederick. *The Life and Work of Auguste Rodin.* London: T. Fisher Unwin, 1906.

Ludovici, Anthony. *Personal Reminiscences of Auguste Rodin.* Philadelphia: J. B. Lippincott, 1926.

Maillard, Leon. *Auguste Rodin, Statuaire.* Paris: H. Floury, 1899.

* Certain editions of this book carried an illustration of a *Dancer* on page 166, from The Museum of Modern Art's Dance and Theater Collection. This drawing, as well as the *Cambodian Dancer* from the City Art Museum of St. Louis (p. 167), are now held to be the work of Ernst Durig.
† Plates 5, 11, 12, 17, and 18 in this book, from the Fogg Art Museum, are now held to be the work of Ernst Durig.

MARX, ROGER. *Auguste Rodin, Céramiste.* Paris: Société de la propagation des livres d'art, 1907.

MAUCLAIR, CAMILLE. *Auguste Rodin, l'homme et l'oeuvre.* Paris: Renaissance du livre, 1918.

RIOTOR, LÉON. *Rodin.* Paris: Félix Alcan, 1927.

ARTICLES

BÉNÉDITE, LÉONCE. "Dante et Rodin." In *Dante: Recueil d'études publiées pour le VIe centenaire du poete.* Paris: Union Intellectuelle Franco-Italienne, 1921, pp. 209–19.

BOIS, GEORGES. "Le Sculpteur Rodin et les danseuses cambodgiennes." *L'Illustration,* No. 3309 (July 28, 1906).

ELSEN, ALBERT. "Rodin's 'La Ronde.'" *Burlington Magazine* (June, 1965), pp. 290–99.

GEISSBUHLER, ELISABETH C. "Rodin's Abstractions—The Architectural Drawings." *Art Journal,* XXIX, No. 1, (1966) 22–30.

GOLDSCHEIDER, CÉCILE. "Rodin et la danse." *Art de France* (1963), pp. 322–35.

GRAUTOFF, OTTO. "Rodins Handzeichnungen." *Kunst und Kunstler* (1908), pp. 218–25.

GSELL, PAULL. "Le Dessin et la couleur." *La Revue,* LXXXVIII, No. 19, (October 1, 1910), 724–29.

"Le Salon National." *L'Art,* No. 35 (1883), p. 38.

MARX, ROGER. "Cartons d'artistes—Auguste Rodin." *L'Image* (September 1897), pp. 293–99.

———. "Les Pointes-sèches de M. Rodin." *Gazette des Beaux-Arts,* XXVII, No. 1 (1902), 204–8.

MAUCLAIR, CAMILLE. "L'Art de M. Auguste Rodin." *Revue des Revues* (June 15, 1898), pp. 597–610.

PARAS-PEREZ, RODOLFO. "Notes on Rodin's Drawings," *The Art Quarterly,* XXX, No. 2 (Summer, 1967).

QUENTIN, CHARLES. "Rodin." *The Art Journal* (July, 1898), pp. 193–96.

ROGER-MARX, CLAUDE. "Engravings by Sculptors in France." *Print Collector's Quarterly,* XVI, No. 2 (April, 1929).

ROSTRUP, HAAVARD. "Dessins de Rodin." *From the Collections of the Ny Carlsberg Glyptothek,* II (1938).

SPECIAL ISSUES OF PERIODICALS DEVOTED TO RODIN, WITH ARTICLES ON HIS DRAWINGS
(in Chronological Order)

La Revue des Beaux-Arts et des Lettres (January 1, 1899).
Revue Populaire des Beaux-Arts (April 8, 1899).
La Plume (June 1, 1899).
Les Maîtres Artistes (October 15, 1903).

L'Art et les Artistes (April, 1914).
Les Arts Français (February, 1918).

LITERARY WORKS ILLUSTRATED WITH RODIN DRAWINGS

BAUDELAIRE, CHARLES. *Les Fleurs du Mal.* New York: Limited Editions Club, 1940 (reproduction of volume illustrated by Rodin in 1888).

BERGERAT, EMILE. *Enguerrande.* Paris: Frinzine, Klein, & Cie., 1884.

CARR, H. D. *Rosa Coeli.* London: Chiswick Press, 1907.

————. *Rosa Inferni.* London: Chiswick Press, 1907.

————. *Rosa Mundi.* London: Chiswick Press, 1905.

CROWLEY, ALEICESTER. *Seven Lithographs by Clot.* Reproduced from the original watercolors of Auguste Rodin, with a chaplet of verse by Aleicester Crowley. London: Chiswick Press, 1907.

GEFFROY, GUSTAVE. *La Vie Artistique.* 2d series. Paris: Dentu, 1893.

HUMILIS. *Les Poèmes d'Humilis.* Paris: Collection "La Poetique", 1910.

MIRBEAU, OCTAVE. *Le Jardin des Supplices.* Paris: Charpentier et Faisquelle, 1899.

————. *Le Jardin des Supplices.* Paris: Vollard, 1902.

OVID. *Les Elegies amoreuses d'Ovide.* Translated by Abbé Bazzin. Paris: Editions Gonin, 1935.

SELECTED REPRODUCTIONS OF AUTHENTIC RODIN DRAWINGS

AUBERT, MARCEL (ed.). *Douze aquarelles inédites de Rodin.* Paris: Librairie des arts decoratifs, 1949.

———— (ed.). *Quatorze aquarelles de Rodin.* Paris: Rene Kieffer, 1933.

DRUET, E. *L'Oeuvre d'Auguste Rodin.* Four volumes of photos in the Cabinet des Estampes, Bibliothèque Nationale, Paris.

GOLDSCHEIDER, CÉCILE (ed.) *Danse—études de Rodin.* Paris: Albert Morancé, 1967.

———— (ed.). *Femmes—Vingt-quatre études de Rodin.* Paris: Albert Morancé, 1966.

———— (ed.). *Rodin—Aquarelles et dessins.* Paris: Albert Morancé, 1963.

GRAPPE, GEORGES (ed.). *Rodin—Dessins.* Paris: Editions Braun, Galerie d'Estampes, 1933.

LA VARENDE, JEAN DE. *Rodin.* Paris: Rombaldi, 1944.

RODIN, AUGUSTE. *Album des peintres-graveurs.* Collection of lithographs with one reproduction of a Rodin drawing by Clot. Paris: Vollard, 1897.

————. *Dix Dessins Choisis.* Reproduced by Boutet. Paris: Au Dépens de l'artiste, 1904.

————. *Germinal.* Collection of lithographs with one reproduction of a Rodin drawing by Clot. Paris: La Maison Moderne, 1899.

————. *Les Dessins d'Auguste Rodin.* With a preface by Octave Mirbeau. Paris: Boussod, Manzi, Joyant, & Cie., 1897.